Helping Young Children Develop Language Skills:

A Book of Activities

Merle B. Karnes

Professor of Special Education
Institute for Research on Exceptional Children
University of Illinois

The Council for Exceptional Children
1411 South Jefferson Davis Highway, Suite 900
Arlington, Virginia 22202

Contents

Preface   vii

I. Listening Skills (Auditory Decoding)   1

Following Verbal Directions with Minimal Verbal Responses   1

Questions Which Can Be Answered with Minimal Verbal
Responses   5

Auditory Discrimination   12

II. Understanding Materials Presented Visually (Visual Decoding) 16

Using Objects, Pictures, and Games to Develop Visual
Perception   16

Learning Concepts through Visual Clues   24

Interpreting Action Pictures   28

Interpreting Actions   29

III. Verbal Expressive Abilities (Vocal Encoding)   31

Verbal Responses to Visual Stimuli   31

Verbal Responses to Auditory Stimuli   34

Games Which Encourage Verbal Responses   37

Simple Problem Solving Which Emphasizes Verbal Responses   39

IV. Motor Expression (Motor Encoding)   **42**

Pantomimes   42
Manipulative Materials   46
Dramatic Play and Free Expression   47
Adaptations for Music Period   52

V. Verbal Associations (Auditory Vocal Association)   **56**

Activities to Reinforce Associations of Opposites or Dissimilar
Qualities   56
Activities to Reinforce Associations of Identical or Similar
Qualities   61
Activities to Reinforce Associations of Class and Category   63
Activities to Reinforce Hypothetical or Inferred Associations   67

VI. Visual Associations (Visual Motor Association)   **71**

Perceiving Similarities and Differences in Material Presented
Visually   71
Perceiving Relationships and Classes in Material Presented
Visually   78
Perceiving Sequential Relationships in Material Presented
Visually   86

VII. Standard Syntactical Constructions and Auditory Closure   **89**
(Auditory Vocal Automatic Process)

Using Concrete Materials to Elicit Verbal Automatic Responses   89
Using Less Concrete Visual Materials to Elicit Verbal Automatic
Responses   92
Using Model Sentences   94
Adapting Word Omission and Sound Blending Techniques   97

VIII. Auditory Memory (Auditory Vocal Sequential Process)   **101**

Recall of Familiar Class Items   101
Recall of More Abstract Items: Digits, Letters, and Rhythms   105
Recall of Songs, Finger Plays, and Nursery Rhymes   107
Recall of Directions   108
Recall of Story Content   109

IX. Visual Memory (Visual Motor Sequential Process)   **111**

Reproduction of Patterns   111
Memory Games with Visual Clues   119

X. Visual Closure   **124**

Appendix: Listing of Sources   **136**

Preface

The activities included in this book were designed by teachers to improve the language skills of culturally disadvantaged preschool children. Over a period of three years these and similar activities have been used with three, four, and five year old disadvantaged children participating in a research project funded by the US Office of Education at the Institute for Research on Exceptional Children, University of Illinois. Children in these experimental groups have generally made significantly greater improvement than have children in a variety of contrast or control groups. Although these activities were developed for use with small groups (of about five) of disadvantaged preschool children, they can be adapted for use with larger groups of more advantaged children or small groups of older children who are mentally retarded or have severe learning disabilities.

The communication processes considered here are derived from the clinical model of the Illinois Test of Psycholinguistic Abilities (ITPA). Although visual closure as a facet of the communication process was not measured by the experimental edition of the ITPA (1961), it is included here and will be assessed in the revision of the ITPA currently underway. The activities in this book, therefore, reflect a language model comprised of five major processes: (a) understanding (decoding), (b) determining relationships (association), (c) closure (integration), (d) expressing ideas (encoding), and (e) memory.

The ITPA can be used to delineate potential strengths and existing weaknesses in the psycholinguistic profile of a given child. His language age score for each of the nine subtests is compared to his chronological age at the time of testing to identify areas which may require remediation. The activities included in this book are, therefore, classified under headings which generally relate to the subtests of the ITPA. Since several aspects of the communication process are usually simultaneously involved, any activity might well have been placed under several different but appropriate headings. Insofar as possible, specific activities were classified according to their *major* language impetus.

The purpose of this book is to familiarize teachers with specific types of activities which can further the development of certain psycholinguistic abilities. This manual is *not* a curriculum; rather, it suggests prototypes through which curricular content may be presented. A teaching style which successfully incorporates these prototypes will effectively emphasize the various aspects of the language process and will insure that a teacher does not rely on only one or two facets of the communication process. Presenting routine curricular material through a number of language processes not only fosters the development of the various processes but also facilitates the learning of the content material.

The author wishes to acknowledge the contributions of Margaret Heggemeir, Laurel Hertig, Audrey Hodgins, Carolyn Lorenz, Jeanne Morris, and Constance Solberg who designed these activities as a part of a workshop on curriculum development for disadvantaged preschool children conducted at the University of Illinois. Finally, the author wishes to thank Samuel A. Kirk, Professor of Special Education and former Director of the Institute for Research on Exceptional Children, University of Illinois, and James J. McCarthy, Associate Professor of Education, Studies in Behavioral Disabilities, University of Wisconsin, both of whom developed the Illinois Test of Psycholinguistic Abilities.

Merle B. Karnes

PART I

Listening Skills

(Auditory Decoding)

Following Verbal Directions with Minimal Verbal Responses

A. Simple Directions. (Demonstrate first when necessary.)

1. Body parts. Begin with singular forms only. Later add plural forms and, later still, randomly mix singular and plural forms: "Touch your ear (eye, nose, head). Touch your ears (eyes, knees, toes)."

2. Music format. Combine body part directions with a simple melody such as "Put Your Finger in the Air."

3. Self introductions. Introduce the children individually to themselves in a full length mirror. "That is Gary Peel. Say, 'Hello, Gary.' Hold out your hand to the boy in the mirror. What is he doing? Put your hand on your head, your shoulder; touch your nose. Does he do everything you do?"

B. Following More Complicated Directions.

1. Do as I say. "This morning, boys and girls, I will see how well you can follow directions. Listen carefully and do just what my sentence tells

you. I may ask *all* of you to do the same thing, or I may call only *one* name."

"Stand behind your chair (in front of, on)" (all children).

"Bring me a book, a piece of chalk, and a pencil" (one child).

"Jump three times and then clap your hands" (all).

"Put a yellow sheet of paper between two red books" (one).

"Stretch up high, touch your toes, and turn around two times" (all).

2. Whispered and "hidden" directions.

a. *Messenger boy.* Choose a child to be the messenger boy and whisper a "message" to him. He chooses a child to receive the message and whispers the message to this child. Sample messages: "Take off one shoe." "Turn around three times." "Stand on one foot." The child who receives the message acts out the request. The other children then guess out loud what they thought the message was. When the children master the game, they can make up their own messages and you will not need to initiate the messages. (This activity involves auditory decoding, motor encoding, visual decoding.)

b. *A mixed-up story.* "I'm going to tell you a story, but you have to listen very closely because every once in a while I'm going to ask one of you to do something. Like this: Once there was a little boy and—(Tony, touch your nose.) Are you ready? Once there was a little boy named Henry. One day his mother said—(Gary, stand up. Good, Gary, you were listening.) One day Henry's mother said, 'I need a loaf of bread from the store and I want you to go to the store for me—(Gloria, scratch your ear.) Here is 25¢. Be sure to—(Raise your hand, Maria.) bring back the change.' Henry was a very careful boy, and he did just what his mother asked him to. But on the way home he saw a friend and said—(Tony, clap your hands.) 'Hi, Joe.' While they were talking, he dropped the money. Joe helped him find it and away he went, taking the bread and money home to his mother.''

3. Games which emphasize directions.

   a. *Chin, chin, chin.* Seat the children in a group facing you. Point to your chin and say, "Chin, chin, chin." Then switch and point to another feature such as your eye but continue to say, "chin." The children must point to what you *say* and not to where you point.

   b. *Simon says.* Begin as Simon and give commands: "Simon says, 'Thumbs up.' Simon says, 'Thumbs down.' '' The children follow the directions. If you give a command without saying "Simon says," the children are not to follow the command. When the children have mastered the game, they may take turns replacing you as Simon.

   c. *Silly relay.* Three or four children are adequate for a relay row. Place everyday items (a chair, hat, mitten, eraser) in a line ahead of the relay row. Give the first child in the row a command series: "Sit on the chair. Put on the cap. Take off the cap. Jump over the mitten." After he completes the series he runs back to his team, taps the next player in line, and goes to the end of the line. Give the second child a different command series which involve the same objects: "Walk around the chair; jump over the cap; put on the mitten; take off the mitten." Continue until each child has had an opportunity to perform a command series. Gradually increase the complexity of the commands.

   d. *I say.* Face the children and act as a captain. When your command fits your action, the children must follow. For example, "I say, touch your feet," and touch your feet. The children must do the same. However, if you say, "I say, bend over," and then raise your arms in the air, the children must remain still and not follow the command.

C. Classroom Activities Which Emphasize Directions.

1. Paper folding. A large piece of construction paper or newsprint can be divided into work areas for pasting and other activities by careful folding. "Pick up the left edge of the paper and bring it over to the right edge. Hold it there while you press the paper flat with your other hand. Good. Now, bring the bottom edges up to the top and then press the paper flat. Has everyone done that? Now, unfold the paper. You can see four rectangles. Let's count them together. We will make a design in each rectangle." (Precut geometric shapes are given each child and he is directed to select certain colored shapes and assemble them in such a way as to have an ice cream cone, a clown, balloons. Of course, the materials pasted, colored, or printed in each rectangle will vary according to the content currently being taught.)

2. Decorating Christmas cookies. After tree shaped cookies have been frosted green by the children, place the decorations (cinnamon dots, silver dots, chocolate chips) on the tables in appropriate containers. Without decorating a tree yourself, give instructions. "Put a silver dot on the top point of your tree. This will be a star for the top of your tree. Put a red cinnamon dot at the end of each branch. How many dots do you need? Put three chocolate chips on the base of your tree. This will make the stand." (To provide an interesting comparison between auditory and visual decoding, have the children decorate a second cookie by example only. Decorate a cookie in a certain way. With no explanation, place your sample before the children and say, "Decorate your cookie just like mine.")

3. Easel and Listening Games, Mary Merwin, (Acadia Press, $5.75 set). Thirty-two easel games are printed on large sheets of paper and may be used on an easel as a group activity. Fifty-two listening games are printed on 8½″ x 11″ paper and are to be completed by individual children. In many instances, a lesson which was performed by the group at the easel is subsequently redone in the smaller format by each child at his desk. Example: "Hold up your red crayon. Keep your red crayon and color one truck red, any one." (Continue until all trucks and then all cars have been colored different colors.) "Touch your red truck. That one must stop. Color the light in front of the truck red. The red light is at the top." Etc.

4. Frostig Visual Perception Program, Follett Educational Corp. Although the major emphasis of these exercises would be in the visual and motor areas (visual decoding, visual closure, visual motor association, visual motor sequential), note that the *directions* are most often given orally by the teacher. Therefore, auditory decoding is a requisite skill for successful completion of the series.

Questions Which Can Be Answered with Minimal Verbal Responses

A. Yes-No-Maybe Questions.

"This morning I am going to read some sentences to you. Listen carefully to each sentence and answer yes, no, or maybe." Suggested content follows:

1. Body image.

Our feet are on the ends of our arms.
You have one head.

Your arm does not bend.
We are sitting down.

2. Immediate environment.

The light is on.
The floor is moving.
We can pick up chairs.

3. Familiar classes or concepts previously taught (fruits, animals, colors, seasons, number, weather, properties of objects).

Grapes grow in bunches.
Bananas are round.
A triangle has four sides.
Horses, cows, and ducks are four legged animals.
A fish can walk.
An ice cream cone is hot.
Bobby is the name of a boy.
Is mud good to eat?
Acorns grow on maple trees.
Leaves turn red and yellow in the fall.
All apples are red.
People turn off their furnaces in the fall.

B. Recall of Simple Items in Sentences and Very Short Stories.

"This morning I shall read some very short stories. Be a good listener. When I finish a story, I shall ask you some questions. If you can answer the questions, then you are a good listener. Ready?"

1. "We have fun in the spring. We jump rope. We play marbles and fly kites.

"What time of the year is it? Name three games we play in the spring."

2. "Today it is raining. We wear our raincoats and hats. Our boots splash in the puddles. We like the spring rain.

"What kind of weather did I mention in the story? What kind of clothes do we wear when it rains?"

3. "I am a baby bird. I live in a nest. I am learning to fly. When I am big, I can sing.

"Where did the baby bird live? What was it learning to do? What will it do when it is a grown up bird?"

4. Tell a story in which children have to remember a specific category, such as color. "There was once a boy named Jack. Jack lived in a *white* house with his mother and father. One day Jack's father brought a dog home for Jack. The dog was *brown*. One day Jack forgot to shut the big *green* door and the dog ran away.

"What was the color of Jack's house? What color was the dog? What color was the big door?"

C. Animal Story.

Select or invent a story that includes the names of familiar animals and that entails repetition of these names. (*The Little Red Hen* is an example.) After the children are seated and ready to listen, assign each child the name of an animal that is in the story and show him how to "talk" like that animal. Whenever you mention his animal in the story, the child must make the sound of the animal.

D. Animal Talk (A game by Mattel, Inc., approximately $5.00).

The red barn with its pull ring produces the sounds of 12 farm animals in a random order. When the ring is pulled, the child responds with the name of the animal which makes that sound. Although the auditory aspect of this game would remain a constant, the response can be changed. A visual response can be required by having the child choose a picture of the correct animal. A motor response can be required by having the child act like the animal whose sound he had heard. A more difficult associative response can be required by having the child choose a related picture, such as a bottle of milk to go with the sound of a cow, a saddle to go with the sound of a horse, an egg to go with the sound of a chicken.

E. Word Omission.

Develop the habit of omitting words which either picture clues or the logic of the material will enable the children to supply. Example:
Story Time. *Peter Johnson and His Guitar*. These questions can be asked after the first reading of the book or during the reading of the story if the children are already familiar with the story. The illustrations help provide the answers. "Peter looked in the _____ (barn). He looked under the _____ (table). He looked behind the _____ (door)."

F. Detection and Correction of Incorrect or Nonsensical Items.

1. Change my sentence. "Today I am going to say some sentences with wrong or silly words in them. Listen to the sentence. If you can change it into a sentence that makes sense, raise your hand." Examples:

> Water is *dry*.
> A nail has a *tail*.
> An ax is an *animal*.
> Cows have four *wings*.
> Jane is the name of a *boy*.
> An apple is *square*.

Ice is *warm*.

A pig can *fly*.

2. Something about you. "I'm going to tell you a silly story about your-selves. Listen very carefully and when you hear something silly, put your hand up.

"Once upon a time, five children came to school. Their names were Debbie, Tony, Maria, Joe, and Derrick. They were all boys and they were all 50 years old. Their teacher was an old man named Grumpy. Every day the children rode to school on a horse. When they got to school, they put on their pajamas and went to bed. When they woke up, they had supper. Then they drew books on the ceiling and took them home. When school was over, a fire engine came to get them."

3. What's wrong here? "I am going to read you a story that has some mis-takes or is funny. Odd things happen. If you hear something that doesn't sound right, raise your hand. When I call on you, tell us what is wrong with the story.

"Once there was a farm right in the middle of town." (If no one raises a hand, ask, "Does anyone know what is wrong with that? Farms are in the country, aren't they? Not in the middle of a town or a city.") "Now I'll read that the right way. Once there was a farm out in the country. The farmer and his wife had *two* children—two girls and a boy. The farmer raised cows, horses, pigs, chickens, and *chairs* on the farm.

"One winter day when it was snowing outdoors, the farmer told his boy to put on his *swimming suit* and go out to feed the horses. When Jimmy reached the barn and opened the door, he could hear the horses calling him, '*Moo, Moo.*' 'They must be very hungry,' thought Jimmy as he rushed over to their stalls. He gave them some *bread* to eat. He also fed the other animals. Then he thought, 'I'll check the chickens' nests and see if they have laid any *buttons* because I sure do like fried *buttons* for breakfast.'

"Jimmy's father came out to the barn and began to milk the *pigs*. After the milking was done, Jimmy and his father could go into the house and have their own breakfast. Jimmy always had *green* milk for breakfast."

G. Riddle Format.

Although there are many inexpensive and suitable books of riddles (*What Am I?*, Golden Press, 35¢; *Riddles, Riddles, from A to Z*, Golden Press, 35¢), you can more effectively use original riddles which relate directly to the subject matter you are teaching.

1. Riddle of class. "I am thinking of a fruit that has a smooth skin. It has a single stone or seed in the center. It is juicy. It grows on a tree. It is purple." Continue providing clues until the children guess that it is a plum.

   "I am thinking of a shape that we often see in buildings. It could be the shape of a brick. It could be the shape of a cement block. It has four sides. The four sides are not all the same length." Continue providing clues until the children guess that it is a rectangle.

   Similar riddles can be made for colors, animals, items of clothing, furniture, and other curricular materials.

2. I see something. "I see something in this room. It is red and it is on the little table. It is a rectangle." Call on a child to name the object (a book). As the children increase in skill, objects which are very familiar but are not actually present in the room can be used. "I am thinking of something. It has four legs, a tail, and it barks. What is it?"

3. Find my child. A child or the teacher plays the part of the mother and one of the children is chosen to be a policeman. The mother tells the policeman that her child is lost and asks him if he will help her find him. The policeman asks if the child is a little boy or girl and what he was wearing when he disappeared. The mother tells the policeman about the clothes. The policeman walks about the room as the clothing is described. When he picks out the child that has on this clothing, he returns him to the mother and another player becomes the policeman. (Auditory decoding, visual decoding, vocal encoding.)

H. Emphasizing Verbal Directions in Teaching Concepts Such as Color.

Example: Establishing names of colors. Poker chips, discs cut from colored posterboard, or painted wooden chips may be used for these activities. Give each child a container with two chips for each of three colors (red, blue, yellow). Pick up a red one: "We want to find one that is the same color. Here it is. Now put them together. Good. Now, find one that is the same color as this one, and put them together. Are these two the same color? Yes, so put them together. Colors have names. I will show you red. (Hold it up.) 'RED!' Everyone hold up a red chip. Good. Mix up your chips. Point to a red one. Good. Say its name. 'RED!' Now I will show you the color yellow. (Hold it up.) 'YELLOW!' Everyone hold up a yellow chip. Say its name. Mix it up with the other colors. Point to a yellow chip; point to a red chip." Repeat until the children do not make mistakes. Then add the blue chips.

The final set of color chips contains eight colors; each new color is introduced in a similar way.

The color shades may be added later. The extremes (light and dark) are introduced first, but children can learn to grade three to five shades of a single color.

Auditory Discrimination

A. Loudness.

Hide a ticking clock while the children close their eyes. The children move about the room quietly to find the clock, aided in their search by the ticking. The finder of the clock becomes the child to hide the clock for the second game.

B. Rhythm.

1. Body movement. When the music plays slowly, the children should move slowly; as it speeds up, so should they. Begin this activity with a drum. Each time you beat it, the children should take a step. At first, the beat will be slow and even. Later, it should be faster and the children should be running. After the drum, piano chords can be used. Finally, musical pieces of increasing complexity can be introduced as the children gain the ability to interpret tempo in music into a corresponding tempo in movement.

2. Rhythm instruments. The children learn to reproduce rhythmic patterns of increasing complexity with a variety of simple instruments. (Hand clapping may be used at first, but the rhythm instruments provide better motivation.) Sample rhythms:

   I
   1-2-3-4   (Instruments struck or sounded on the first beat only.)

   I   I
   1-2-3-4   (On the first and third beats.)

   I υ I υ
   1-2-3-4   (A long sound on beats one and three and a short sound on beats two and four.)

   Teach variations with combinations of loud-soft or of skipped beats.

Similar variations may be introduced with a 1-2-3 rhythm. When the children are able to maintain the rhythm, a piano melody may be super-imposed. Unison counting helps to maintain the rhythm.

C. Tone.

1. Piano scales. "My fingers can walk up the piano." (Play the scale.) "Can you hear them? Now what happened?" (Slide down the scale.)
   Play scale slowly. "Am I walking or running? Am I going up or down?" "Am I playing loudly or softly?"

2. Resonator bells (Creative Playthings, DM 245, $15.95). Each bell is mounted on a separate block, comes with its own mallet, and can be used individually. These eight bells present the diatonic scale Middle C to C.
   Initially present only two bells to the child and ask him to select the higher and lower sound. As his acuity in auditory discrimination develops increase the number of bells presented. Ideally, a child would be able to arrange the eight in order of a chromatic scale, but such a performance would not be required of all children. Skill in arranging four or five bells would be considered an adequate performance.
   The idea of matching sounds (same or like sounds and different sounds) can also be taught if a double set of bells is available.

D. Identifying Everyday Sounds.

1. Classroom tapes. Make a tape recording of various ordinary sounds: the piano, drum, door shutting, children clapping, someone walking, water running, a teacher talking, etc. Leave a space after each sound for the children to identify it: "Listen closely to the sounds. If you know what any of them are, raise your hand. Close your eyes and tell me what this sound is." (Draw a chair on the floor.) "All right, open your eyes. What

was it?" If the children have the idea, start the tape. If they don't, try other examples before using the tape.

2. Sounds I Hear (Four 33 1/3 rpm records—$16.50 the set;—Scott Foresman and Co.). "Sounds around the House," "Sounds around the Farm," "Sounds in the Zoo," "Sounds around the Neighborhood," and "Sounds around the School." These records may be used with or without the accompanying picture card photographs as a visual aid. This set is useful for combining auditory discrimination with oral expression.

E. Discerning Rhyming Words.

1. Riddle-a-Rhyme Lotto (Childcraft Equipment Co., $1.00). The game contains 6 playing boards and 48 pictures for riddles and rhyming. Read the riddle rhymes aloud and allow the children to provide the rhyming answer and the correct picture for the lotto board. Example:

> "It's made of wood
> And rhymes with hat.
> To hit a baseball
> You need a ——."

A child responds with the word "bat" and finds the correct picture card to place on the lotto board.

2. *Kindergarten Rhymes,* by Mary Jackson Ellis (Teachers Publishing Corp., 70003, $6.95). One hundred cut outs and a 48 page book of rhymes appropriate to the pictures are included. Examples:

> "I met a *toad*   (The italicized words have accompanying pictures.)
> On a *road*"

> "See a *hen*
> In a *pen*"

This set may be used in a variety of ways. Some variations are as follows:

a. Ask the children to supply the second rhyming word. A visual clue may be given (the child choosing the correct word from four or five pictures), but the child may also be asked to provide a rhyming word without a picture clue. When pictures are provided, you may ask the child to choose pictures for both rhyming words.

b. Place the rhyming word pictures in pairs on the table; include some pairs which do not rhyme. Ask the children to name the pairs which rhyme and to take out those which do not rhyme.

c. You may provide rhyming riddles for the pictures: "I am thinking of an animal. It has four legs. It has a long tail. It rhymes with hat" (i.e., cat or rat).

d. Place the rhyming pictures at random on the flannel board. A child chooses one picture and then looks for another picture which rhymes with the first one he chose. He then repeats both words and places the pair side by side on the chalk ledge.

3. Which pictures rhyme? "Can you think of two words that rhyme? Good, 'cat' and 'hat' rhyme. 'Pie' and 'tie' rhyme. Here is a worksheet with some pictures on it. Each picture has a rhyming partner. Mark the rhyming partners with the same crayon. Don't use the same color for more than two pictures." (Examples: hat-cat; spoon-moon; pen-hen; car-star.)

4. Rhyming pictures for felt board (Beckley-Cardy Co., Instructo No. 32, $2.50). These pictures may be adapted for a variety of activities, as in 2 above.

PART II

Understanding Materials Presented Visually

(Visual Decoding)

Using Objects, Pictures, and Games to Develop Visual Perception

A. Matching Games.

1. Perception Plaques (Creative Playthings, A389 Perception Faces, Differences in facial features, $4.50; A390 Perception Clowns, Differences in body features, $4.50). Twelve pairs of plywood plaques (2³/₈″ square) with similar designs may be used in group or solitary matching games. Rather precise visual discrimination is required.

2. Picture Dominoes (Beckley-Cardy Co., No. 102, $1.25). Picture dominoes can be used to teach matching as a group or solitary game.

3. Forest Friends (Milton Bradley Co., No. 4808, $1.00). Players match the animal pictures on the big spinner with identical pictures on the game board. The object is to reach the end of the forest path.

4. Picture Readiness Game (Garrard Publishing Co., $1.75). A lotto game

in which the match made is an exact one. There is a classifying factor since each playing card represents a different category (fruits, for instance).

5. Spots and Stripes (Arrco Playing Card Co., 29¢). This is an expensive, attractively designed game which is played in a fashion similar to dominoes. If a player is unable to match the required number of spots or stripes he may use a wild card—a tiger or zebra for the needed stripes, a leopard or a giraffe for the needed spots—if he is lucky enough to draw a wild card.

6. Candy Land (Milton Bradley Co., Deluxe Edition, No. 4403, $3.00). No reading or arithmetic is required to play this game. Each child draws a card and moves his playing piece to the corresponding color or object square on the game board.

7. Chicken Lotto (Penney's stores, No. X923-4550A, $2.22). In this color game, players press down on the chicken's tail to receive a colored egg. The lotto boards which accompany this game are not suitable for young children. Use small plastic pans or paper cups for the color sorting.

8. Nature Cards (McGraw-Hill—6 titles, 3″ x 6″; from Beckley-Cardy Co., $1.10 each, or from Creative Playthings—bird, flower, and animal cards edited by Roger Tory Peterson—set of 3, S775, $3.00). Purchase these or similar cards in sets of two. Initially a child matches identical pictures: one grasshopper and another grasshopper, one beetle and another beetle, one robin and another robin, one cardinal and another cardinal. Later subjects may be combined and the child instructed to sort out all the insects, all the birds, etc., depending upon the collection. The McGraw-Hill collection is particularly well done with excellent, realistic pictures and is a large size which is easy for the children to see and handle.

9. Wildlife Old Maid (National Wildlife Federation, 20033, $1.00). Play this game at first as a simple sorting game. When the children have become familiar with the cards and understand the principle of likeness, they may play a traditional form of Old Maid with the cards. The quality of illustration makes these cards superior to the ordinary Old Maid purchased in the dime store. The fish, birds, and other animals pictured on these cards are more useful for classroom purposes than the usual comic characters.

10. Wood Lotto (Creative Playthings, AA335, $4.95). Thirty-six small wooden plaques are matched to corresponding pictures on six master boards.

    There are other useful and inexpensive lotto games available at bookstores and toy departments. Beckley-Cardy Co. offers Zoo Lotto, Farm Lotto, Object Lotto, World About Us Lotto, and Go-Together Lotto at $1.25 a set.

B. Simple Objects and Pictures.

1. Picture Shape Puzzles. Mount small catalog and magazine pictures which show an everyday object with a familiar geometric shape. Examples: a cracker, clock, or cushion in a circle shape; a window or table in rectangular shape. Direct the children to sort these pictures by shape. Each child may monitor a specific shape or the sorting may be done in piles in the center of the table.

2. Object sorting. Use muffin pans, egg cartons, small plastic containers, small aluminum pie pans, or paper cups for sorting activities. Dried seeds make an excellent early sorting activity. The seed assortment might contain kidney beans, lima beans, calico beans, northern beans, and pop corn (unpopped). Safety pins, nails, and screws of different

sizes may also be sorted. Buttons may be sorted by size and color. Wooden beads may be sorted by shape and color. Advanced sorting may require the child to put one bead (or whatever is being sorted) in the first muffin cup, two in the second, etc., up to six.

3. Finding identical pictures. Prepare simple mimeographed sheets which show an array of similar objects. Instruct each child to find two which are the same. Examples: two identical fish among six assorted spotted and striped fish, two identical birthday cakes among an assortment with different decorations and number of candles, two identical flowers among an assortment of flowers.

4. Copying designs in bead stringing. Give each child beads and a lace in a small container. "Can you make a necklace just like mine? Watch me. A red bead, a yellow bead. Can you do that? Good. Let's try it again. A red bead, a yellow bead." Later, prepare a different bead pattern on a lace (knotted at both ends) for each child. Can he copy this pattern by himself, checking for accuracy as he peforms the task?

5. Other designs. Make a row with four colored candies: red, green, red, yellow. Give each child an assortment of candies to choose from. Can he make the same pattern under yours?

    Make a simple design with five candies. Give the child the exact number of items he needs to copy it. Can he reproduce the figure?

Examples:

```
X                    X   X
X                        X
X X X                X       X
```

Later, give each child more candies than he needs to copy the design. Does he copy the pattern one for one, or does he attempt to reproduce the pattern using all of the candies?

Activities similar to those above can be structured from a variety of materials: poker chips, wooden beads, oyster crackers, or felt pieces and a felt board.

6. Place setting. Set up a model place setting: mat, plate, knife, fork, and spoon. Give each child the necessary items. "Set your table like mine." Cups, glasses, or napkins may be added later. Doll dishes and play silverware may be used.

7. Proceeding from actual objects to less concrete presentations. When a real object is used, children are often able to employ different senses in becoming acquainted with the object and are able to use many clues for identification. A progressive sequence toward abstraction might proceed something like this:

   a. Examination of actual fruit (or whatever items are currently under examination).

   b. Identification of a realistic picture of the fruit—a simple picture without other distracting elements.

   c. Identification of a realistically colored silhouette.

   d. Identification of a realistically colored silhouette of the fruit mounted on black paper and folded down the center. The child identifies the fruit from the half silhouette and then unfolds the silhouette to check his response. (This is actually a visual closure activity, but it fits logically in this progression.)

   e. Identification of a black silhouette of the fruit (no color clue).

   f. Identification of the fruit from a dotted outline only. These outlines may be mimeographed if the children are to follow the dots with a pencil or crayon. However, children may identify these shapes without actually drawing on the lines. (Again, this is more properly a visual closure activity.)

g. Identification of the fruit in a picture which has other elements or which has the fruit in a slightly changed form. (Cherries in a cherry pie, grapes in a bowl of assorted fruit, lemons cut into wedges, strawberries in strawberry shortcake).

8. Object picture match. Collect everyday items (a sock, hat, fork, pair of glasses, pencil, comb, etc.) in a box. "We will pass this box around the table. Each of you take out one thing and then tell us what it is. Now I'm going to pass around another box with pictures in it. Find the picture that has the same thing on it as you just picked out of the other box."

9. "I see." Say, "I see a _____" and point to an object. The children provide the name of the object. Soon, they may be able to say the name of the object and its color or what it is made out of. "I see a pink chair"; "I see a wooden pencil."

10. Look and tell. Put a collection of everyday objects in the center of the table. Provide a question clue and ask the children to pick the right object. Examples:

tin foil plate	"What's round and shiny?"
knitting needle	"What's long and sharp?"
toothpick	"What's short and sharp?"
piece of fur	"What's fuzzy?"
bottle opener	"What do you open pop with?"
chalk	"What do you write on the board with?"
pencil	"What do you write on paper with?"

ring	"What do you wear on your finger?"
necklace	"What do you wear around your neck?"

11. Presenting new equipment or reviewing old materials. When you are introducing new materials, place the needed equipment on the table. Point to an object and ask a child what it is. If no child knows the name of the object, provide its name and ask each child to repeat it. With familiar materials, ask the children to identify the materials (felt board, poker chips, pencils, chalk, rods, etc.) and to tell you what we do with it at school.

12. Sightseeing trips. Take a walk around the immediate neighborhood. Tell the children before you leave that they are going to try to see and remember as many things as they can. Choose one child at a time to point out all the things he sees and name them. The teacher should provide an example: "I see a tall tree. I see the sidewalk. I see the light-post. I see the grass." Encourage the children to see increasingly smaller or less conspicuous objects on subsequent trips (the cracks in the side-walk, a paper cup in the gutter, clouds in the sky, house numbers).

13. Who's missing? Direct one child to turn his back to the group and to cover his eyes. Point to another child to leave the room. The remaining children quietly switch their positions. When "it" turns around and faces the group he must try to guess who is missing before the other children count to five slowly. The game is repeated with a new "it."

14. Color slides. Slides taken of the children during field trips or while they are participating in ordinary school routines can be used later for specific visual tasks. These color slides will also stimulate verbal responses and recall.

15. Catalog pointing. Provide a large catalog. Each child takes turns opening it at random and pointing to an object. He then identifies that object (chair, dishes, hat, shoes, lamps).

16. During ordinary storytime periods, give special emphasis to pictures. Use them at times to help the children predict what will happen in the story; at other times use the pictures to help the children recall what has happened earlier in the story. This can also be done by the children as a way of telling the story themselves without the teacher reading the story. Many picture books have such detailed pictures that if the children describe the pictures on each page, the story becomes quite clear.

17. Detective. Materials required are a sand table or a plastic dishpan filled with damp sand and a collection of objects with which to make "tracks" (a cork, pop bottle cap, pencil, cup, small cookie cutters, fork). Direct the children to close their eyes while you make tracks with one of the objects in the sand. The children must then decide which object was used to leave the trail. (This activity can be elaborated upon during storytime with some of the excellent children's books available on animal footprints.)

18. My shadow. Materials required are child size pieces of wrapping paper and black felt tipped markers. Place a piece of wrapping paper on the floor. Direct a child to lie down on the paper and trace his outline with the felt marker, taking care to include details like five fingers, shoe laces, and special identifying outlines such as pigtails. Hang the outline picture on the wall at floor level so that the child may closely compare himself with his outline. Later the child may add with crayons his features and his clothing. The items of clothing should be made to correspond in color with the clothing the child is wearing that day.

Learning Concepts through Visual Clues

A. Geometric Shapes.

1. Colored masonite geometric shapes (The Judy Company, $1.50 for 3 doz., or can be homemade from colored posterboard) may be used for a variety of matching and sorting activities. "Find a shape like the one I am holding. Which square is blue? Which shape is an oval? Which oval is orange? Find a shape like this one which is not red. Mary, find all the yellow shapes; Tod, find all the red shapes."

2. Shapes at juice time. Cut napkin silhouettes in basic shapes and provide crackers in assorted shapes. Children may serve themselves by finding crackers to match the shape of their napkin (two triangular crackers to go with a triangular napkin).

B. A Color Game.

1. Provide three shades of six colors in a pile in front of the dealer. (Painted wooden chips may be used or strips of colored paper may be reinforced with cardboard.) "We are going to play a game. I will be the dealer first, and when I make a mistake, it will be Gary's turn. Now each choose a color which you will collect. You will take turns asking the dealer for your color. The dealer will find that color and give it to you. If he makes a mistake, the next person is the dealer. Are you ready? All right, Gloria, which color do you need?" (The teacher makes a "mistake" as soon as the children have learned the routine of the game.) An earlier version of this game might use five or six paper strips of the same color. Another version might use a box of assorted colored objects. One child collects all the red objects (a comb, airplane, block, toothbrush); another child collects all the blue objects (a plastic flower, cup, scarf, crayon).

C. Position.

1. Open or closed. Collect in a folder mounted pictures of paired items which are shown open or shut: refrigerators, stoves, boxes, doors, books, bottles. Ask a child to pick out those items which are open, those that are closed. Later, the children may identify and place the pairs side by side: an open book, a closed book; an open car door, a closed car door.

2. Suggestions for similar picture folders might include up and down, in or out, in front of or in back of, night and day, summer and winter, city and country, big and little.

D. Number.

1. Singular and plural. Provide pictures or simple blackboard sketches of single and multiple items. Each child selects a picture and identifies it. Help him to structure a sentence which will emphasize singular and plural forms.

   Examples:

I see one shoe.	or	I see two shoes.
I see one foot.	or	I see two feet.
I have one dog.	or	I have three dogs.

   Felt boards and felt shapes (animals, stars, circles) may also be used to emphasize singular and plural forms.

2. Collecting pictures by number. Assign each child a number from one to five. When you hold up a picture of two shoes, the child assigned the number "two" says: "May I have the picture of two shoes?" Allow time for the child to count. Accept a variety of requests but encourage each child to use plural forms in his request.

Learning concepts through visual clues.

E. Size.

1. Size and order. Distribute a work sheet to each child or draw simple sketches at the board to provide a group lesson. "This morning I am going to see how well you can follow directions. Get out your crayons because you will be making marks on the worksheet I will give you. Now, how many dogs (or some other appropriate object) do you see? Are they all the same size? Look at the dogs carefully and mark them when I give you the directions. Ready?

"Put a red mark on the biggest dog.
Put a blue mark on the smallest dog.
Put a green mark on the first dog.
Put a brown mark on the third dog.
Put a black mark on the second dog.
Put an orange mark on the last dog."

2. Size and color. In a box or plastic dishpan place paired objects which are identical except for one aspect: Large and small milk cartons, large and small paper cups, red and green paper cups, a red and a green plastic spoon, a long and a short pencil, a large and a small comb. "Tell me why I have these two together. Now, tell me how this one is different from that one." Later allow the children to pick a pair for themselves. "Why do those two belong together? How are they different?"

F. Names.

1. Place cards. Print each child's name on a cardboard strip. Before the children sit at the table, distribute these place cards randomly about the table. "Look at the name cards and see if you can find yours. Then sit down at that place. If you can't find your name, I will help you." Later the children can hang their coats on hooks which have name cards or identify their paper cup at juice time because of a printed name label.

2. Name chart for assigning coat hooks. Make a chart with all the children's names on it and a slot into which the teacher can place a colored shape or other identifying mark, such as a flower or animal seal. Corresponding colored shapes are pasted above the hooks for the children's coats. As each child comes in, the teacher helps him find his name on the chart and his colored shape. The child then finds the corresponding shape over the hook and hangs his coat there.

   Each month the colored shapes should be changed on the name chart so that the child must make a new association.

G. **Frostig Visual Perception Program (Follett Educational Corp., approximately $96).**

Although other ITPA areas are involved in completing the Frostig sheets (auditory decoding, visual motor association, visual motor sequential, and visual closure), much of the work would emphasize general visual decoding.

Interpreting Action Pictures

A. **Simple, Independent Pictures.**

1. Simple actions. Mount and keep in a folder a collection of simple action pictures. "Tell me about this picture. What are the children doing? Where are they? How many children are there? Are they boys or girls?"

2. Simple moods. Mount and keep in a folder a collection of pictures of children with vivid facial expressions. "Look at the child in this picture. Do you think he is happy or sad? Why do you think he is feeling that way?"

B. **Pictures from Familiar Stories.**

Order an extra copy of inexpensive books so that you can cut and mount key pictures. Example:

The Gingerbread Man: "Here is a picture from a story that you know. Can anyone tell me the name of the story? Good. Now tell me what is happening in the picture. Can you take these three pictures and show me what happened to the gingerbread man first? What happened next? What happened last?"

C. Detecting Bizarre or Missing Elements.

Draw simple pictures at the blackboard with obvious mistakes: a child in a swimming suit playing in the snow, a cat in a fish bowl, an elephant in a tree, a child sitting down to eat at a table which is upside down. "Look at this picture carefully. Do you see anything that is wrong with it? Tell me how I should change this picture."

Interpreting Actions

A. Touching Exercises.

Direct the children to observe, to imitate, and then to verbalize the actions. Touch your head. The children touch their heads and say: "I touch my head." Touch your eye, etc.

B. Following Directions Given in Actions.

"We are going to make a little book. Do just what I do." Give each child a large sheet of paper. "Are you ready?" Fold the paper in half along the long dimension of the paper. If all the children have followed, fold the paper again in the same direction. Check to see if all the children have followed. Unfold the paper and show the class the four long rectangles which the creases have made. Hand out scissors. "Now watch where I cut." Cut the rectangles apart. Stack the rectangles evenly and fold them in half along the short side. After all the children have reached this point, staple the pages together along the center crease. The book is ready for drawing or pasting work.

C. Pantomimes.

1. Action bingo. Place a row of pictures of familiar animals on the table. Give each child several buttons or poker chips. "Gloria will be first. I will whisper the name of an animal in her ear, and she will then act or move like that animal. If you guess the name of the animal, put a button on that picture. When you have three cards with buttons, it will be your turn." The pictures, of course, need not be animals but could represent familiar actions: riding a bike, driving a car, sweeping the floor.

2. Nursery rhymes and simple stories. Select a rhyme or short story with which the children are familiar. Teach the children simple actions to suit the story; *The Three Bears,* for instance, allows for simple, repetitive actions which are easily learned by young children. A few simple props will encourage actions initially. Encourage visual decoding by asking the children to interpret the actions: "What is Tony (Father Bear) doing *now*?"

3. Action songs or finger plays. Familiar songs such as "The Wheels on the Bus" or "Put Your Finger in the Air" encourage motor responses. Visual decoding may be encouraged by directing certain children to act out a stanza before it is sung and asking another child what we should now sing. "What is Joe showing us? Yes, the horn on the bus goes toot, toot, toot. Let's sing about it now."

PART III

Verbal Expressive Abilities

(Vocal Encoding)

Verbal Responses to Visual Stimuli

A. Show and Tell.

A child brings an object from home to share with the group. Help him to talk freely if he can but prompt him when necessary:

"Can you tell me one thing about your book?
Can you tell me two things about your book?
What color is the cover?
Who reads it to you?"

Prompt the child until he has told as many things about the object as he can.

Although the traditional show and tell is a verbal activity, it can become a tasteless sort of competition with toys and other personal belongings. In addition, the format is monotonous. Once begun, show and tell is often impossible to stop and it drags on for weeks and months and even years— into the second grade! Improvisation of the show and tell format is a safer bet. When the children are grouped in a circle, ask one question which each child takes turns answering. ("What did you do on Sunday when we were not in school? Stand up and tell us what the person next to you is wearing today. What do you like to do most when you are all by yourself and have no one to play with? Tell us what your house looks like. Tell us one thing about the bus that brings you to school.") At first the teacher will have to prompt the children with more detailed followup questions or the response will be only a word or two.

B. Choose and Tell.

1. Pick a page. Place a large Sears, Roebuck and Co. catalog on the piano bench. Call a child to come up and open the book to a page at random. The child then chooses some object on that page to tell the class about. ("What color is it? Who uses it? Where would you keep it? What does it do or what is it for? What is it made out of?")

2. Pick and talk box. A variety of everyday items are kept in a box and changed from time to time. The children gather in a circle. One child at a time picks an item from the box and tells about it. To avoid difficulty in choosing, hold the box high or put a cloth over the top so that the object chosen is a surprise to everyone. Sample items: a hair pin, ear muffs, penny, hairnet, paperclip, earring, candle, eye dropper, crayon, clothes pin, bottle opener.

3. Grab bag. Items are taken by the children one at a time from a covered container. Each child tells what he has in as much detail as possible. Examples:

   Place an assortment of fruit in a sack. A child picks out an orange. ("It is round. It is orange. It has seeds. It is juicy. It is sweet. It grows on a tree. I like it.")

   An assortment of cardboard geometric shapes are placed in a box. A child draws a green triangle. ("It has three sides. It is green. It looks like the roof of a house. It is called a triangle.")

   Later this game can be made more difficult if the child does not show his item to the class but merely tells about it until they can guess what he chose.

4. Pick a card (Beckley-Cardy Co., Nature Cards, by McGraw-Hill, 6 titles, 3" x 6", $1.10 each). Animal, bird, or insect cards may be used. A child draws a card from a selection which is face down on the table. "Tell me three things about the card you have drawn." (The number requested may be raised when the children gain proficiency in this task.) Responses could be: "It has two legs. It flies. It lays eggs. It is blue. It eats worms."

5. Pick a picture. Collect simple action pictures and allow each child to select one. "Pick out a picture that makes you think of something. Tell us what it makes you think of. Make up a little story about those people (or animals)." Help the child with questions and suggestions.

6. Picture dictionaries. *The Cat in the Hat Dictionary* and *The Little Golden Dictionary* (plus many others) are suitable to use in motivating vocal responses. The child picks a picture to tell about. His description is supplemented by the teacher who reads what the dictionary has to say about that particular entry after the child has finished.

7. Books. Classification books like *The Big Book of Trucks, The Train Book, The Wonder Book of Trucks,* or *The Golden Book of Boats* are useful in eliciting vocal responses. As the children go through the book they can take turns telling all about one particular kind of truck—a garbage truck, a mail truck, etc. The McGraw-Hill Panorama books are also useful for similar activities. These books are made of very heavy cardboard and fold outward and stand up by themselves. The children may take turns telling about each page.

8. What Is It? Tell Me About It. Cut out pictures or use commercially available sets for the felt board such as those made by Instructo and avail-

able from Beckley-Cardy Co. "Today I shall give each one of you a picture. Look at it carefully and think of all the things you can say about it. Raise your hand when you are ready to tell the class about your picture. You may come up to the front of the room and put your picture on the flannel board. Let's see who can tell the most about his picture."

9. Paint a Picture and Tell a Story. "One of the things so many of you enjoy doing when you have some free time is painting. You have made such interesting looking pictures, and I am sure those pictures would help you tell the class a good story. I think we have time for about three stories today. Who would like to be first?"

10. Know Your Fruit. Use a bowl of real or artificial fruit; vary the content of this activity according to what you are currently teaching. "I know you can all name the fruit I have in this bowl, but I wonder how much you know about each piece of fruit. Let's start with the apple. Think of all the things you know about apples while I draw a picture of an apple on the board. Each time you tell me something about the apple, I'll put a mark under the apple picture. We'll do the same thing for each piece of fruit we talk about today. When we finish we'll count the marks. If I put many marks under the picture of the apple, what will that tell us? If I put only a few marks, what will that tell us?"

Verbal Responses to Auditory Stimuli

A. Tell Me What You Want.

Encourage the children at first and later insist that they verbalize their wants and needs. When a child pokes you and holds up his paper, ask: "What do you want?" At juice time elicit a comment on the type of juice or the shape of the cracker. Do not tie the child's shoe merely because he points to his foot or sticks it out.

B. Tell Us What You Did.

Devote a few minutes, possibly at the beginning of the school day, to encouraging the children to tell about something which happened to them that day or the day before. "What did you have for lunch? What did you do after school yesterday? Who is your best friend? Did you see a good program on television last night? Tell me something you saw on the way home from school."

C. Do What I say.

Choose a child and whisper a set of instructions to him. "Go to the door, open it, close it, and come back to your chair." Verbal responses are involved when you ask the other children to describe what the chosen child did. The child who can name all of the activities performed is chosen next. This can be an effective game if you suggest rather interesting and unusual things: sit on the table, peek through your legs, etc. The children want to perform next and, therefore, watch carefully so they can do a good job of describing what they have seen.

D. Give Us a Hint.

Ask each child to think of something for us to guess (or he can choose an item from a collection and conceal it from the others). Each child gives hints about the item until the others can guess.

E. What Do You Like to Do Best?

"I want you to think about the things you like to do best, the things you like to do at home and the things you like to do at school. What do you like to do best, Gary? Is that at home or at school? What do you like to do best, Darlene?" Vary the question: favorite colors, favorite foods, favorite animals.

F. Tell Us What to Do.

When the children are repeating familiar activities, encourage them to provide the directions or the rules. When reviewing after a class period or on subsequent days, ask the children to "tell us exactly what we did." For example: show the children how to make Christmas wreaths by tracing large plastic coffee can lids with a green crayon and coloring the circle green. Red berries may be added with a red crayon; a small red bow (teacher made) from wrapping ribbon may be stapled on. Cut out the wreath and cut a circle from the center. Hang the wreaths over the ends of branches of the Christmas tree or use them as room decorations. The next day: "Don't our Christmas wreaths look pretty? Who can tell me how we made them? Does anyone remember what we did?" Continue to question for specific details.

G. Differences and Likenesses.

Collect items in related pairs: two balls—one big ball, one little ball; two clothes pins—one pinch and one snap on; two shoelaces—one plaid and one brown or one long and one short. Question: "What do you have?" Answer: "Two balls." Question: "How are they different?" Answer: "One is big." Vary the questions according to the items and increase the specific detail requested.

Games Which Encourage Verbal Responses

A. Let's Pretend to Be the Teacher.

"Would you all like to pretend to be the teacher for a little while? You will have to tell us how to do something, such as coloring circles, putting on a coat, making steps with the short and tall blocks, making a poker chip design. What would you like to teach us, Gloria?" Offer suggestions if the children need help at first.

B. Guess Who.

"Let's pretend to be animals in a zoo, but don't tell anyone your name! We will just tell something about ourselves and see if anyone can guess our names. Like this: I am a large animal with four legs. I have a very pretty coat with black and white stripes. Can you guess my name?" If no one guesses "zebra," continue. "I look a lot like a horse. Yes, Gary, I am a zebra. Now it is your turn to describe the animal you are going to pretend to be."

C. Let's Pretend to Be Animals on a Farm.

"Today we are going to be farm animals. We need a farmer to take care of us. Who wants to be the farmer? All right, Joe, you will be the farmer. I'll come around the table and you whisper which animal you are going to be and the sound that animal makes. Good. Everybody knows which animal he is. Now, let's pretend we are hungry and we want the farmer to feed us. We will use our animal voices to call him. The farmer will walk around the table and you 'moo' or 'cackle.' The farmer will call your name and say, 'Here is your food.' All right, farmer, you had better feed your animals!"

D. Tell Us What to Do.

Put a child in charge of a routine activity—a familiar song, for instance. Since many of the songs four year olds learn involve motor responses, let the leader direct the group. Encourage him to improvise new verses:

"This is the way we trace in school. . . ."
"This is the way we drink our juice. . . ."

(to the tune of "Here We Go 'Round the Mulberry Bush")

E. Guess What I Am Looking At.

Initially you will supply the clues; later, the children can make up examples. Slowly describe an object in the classroom until the children are able to guess what it is. "It is made of metal. It is red. It has a handle. It is on the wall. It has little holes in it. You put a pencil in one of the holes. You sharpen a pencil with it."

F. Guess What I Am Thinking Of.

This game proceeds much as the one described above (E). However, this time you may suggest a class of objects in order to help define the responses. Example: Food. The children take turns describing a food while the other children try to guess what food he is thinking of. "It is yellow. I put butter on it. Sometimes it comes in a can. Then I eat it with a spoon. It is corn." Other categories: colors, items of furniture, animals, etc.

G. Lotto Games.

Although lotto games emphasize visual perceptions, verbal responses can be built into the game and insisted upon.

"May I have the picture of grapes."
"I need the red circle."
"Who is collecting animal pictures?"
"Who needs a chair?"

Simple Problem Solving Which Emphasizes Verbal Responses

A. Telling a Story.

Show a simple picture to the child, a crying baby in a playpen, for instance. Ask leading questions to get the child thinking: "Is the baby happy? How can you tell? What do you think made him cry?" Pictures can increase in complexity as the child's ability to generate interpretations increases.

B. Completing a Story.

Begin a simple action story on a familiar theme. Ask for and utilize suggestions: "What do you think happened next?" Continue the story as long as it moves without too much difficulty.

C. Presenting Children with a Series of Pictures.

Have a child arrange a series of pictures to make a story. At first three pictures represent a maximum. When the pictures are arranged, the child tells the story. Examples: a boy preparing dog food, a dog eating; mother preparing food, a family eating; a snowy scene, a man shoveling snow. A simple comic strip like "Nancy" may be used after it has been mounted on lightweight cardboard.

D. Can You Tell Me Why . . .

You wore boots today?
The icicle melted?
We have stop signs at corners?
We keep the puzzles in a rack?
We keep the books on a shelf?

E. What Will We See If . . .

We go to a farm?
We go to the IGA?
We go outside after supper?
We come to school?

F. Why Do We . . .

Wash our hands?
Pour juice to that line?
Walk slowly with cookies on a tray?
Put books back on the shelf?
Come to school?

G. Tell Me How . . .

You brush your teeth.
You get home from school.
Your mother peels potatoes.
You should cross the street.

H. Tell Me Where . . .

You buy shoelaces.

You hang up your coat.
You get your hair cut.
You sleep at night.

I. **Tell Me What You Have.**

Give each child several small pictures cut from magazines and mounted on cardboard. Ask leading identification questions which will help the child identify the picture card you have in mind. "Who has a picture of a *red* car?" After the correct picture has been located, ask specific questions of the child who holds it. "How many children are in the car? Who is driving? Are they driving in the city or the country? How do you know?"

PART IV

Motor Expression

(Motor Encoding)

Pantomimes

A. I Am Your Mirror.

Seat the children in front of you. "I am your mirror. Look at me. Do what I do." Make a gesture, a facial expression, etc., and have the children follow your action.

B. What Am I Doing?

Whisper to a child a simple action to perform. He acts out the suggestion and his classmates guess what he is doing. Examples: washing dishes, getting dressed, eating, patting a dog, reading, sweeping, cooking, rocking a baby, hanging clothes on the line.

C. Animal Walk.

Although a number of children's records are available on this theme, at first work with the children yourself and help them to develop an acceptable motor response for each animal. The record will proceed too rapidly and without enough repetition for young children, and confusion will result. An elephant walk can be taught as a slow walk with the head forward and the arms together, swinging from side to side like a trunk. A cat can walk very, very quietly. As the children become familiar with more domestic and wild animals, the repertoire can be enlarged. (Birds can flap, bunnies can hop, storks can stand on one leg.)

D. What Animal Am I?

One or two children act out the movements of various animals. The others guess or identify the animal. Suggest relatively simple actions: an elephant with a swinging trunk; the flapping wings of a bird; rabbits hopping; turtles plodding along. A set of pictures may be used to limit the choices and to help the audience make the identification.

E. What Can You Do?

Each child selects a picture of an everyday object from a box and demonstrates the use of whatever he draws. Example: Selecting a picture of a pair of boots, the child could act out putting on the boots. Selecting a picture of a hammer, the child can demonstrate pounding.

The game can also be played by substituting animal pictures in the box. Now the children imitate the animals (gallop like a horse, waddle like a duck, flap like a bird). Be sure that the children have a clear concept of the animals included in this collection.

F. How Would You Walk?

Ask the children, either as a group or by taking turns: "How would you walk if you were an old man with a cane, a baby, a giant, a lady in high heels, a boy in boots that are too big, if you were walking on ice, walking in deep snow, walking in sticky mud, walking against a very strong wind, walking with one broken leg?"

G. Do What I Say.

Adapt a simple command formula to many routine group activities. For example, on the playground, line up the group for a relay and give brief commands to each in turn: "Roll the ball to me. Bounce the ball to me. Toss the ball to me. Throw the ball between your legs. Throw the ball to your friend."

H. Household Pantomime.

At first introduce actual household items to familiarize the children with their operation. Later, ask them to pantomime that operation. Sample items and operations: an egg beater, a hammer, a screw driver, stirring with a spoon, swatting flies, ironing clothes, drying dishes, pouring from a bottle, setting the table, sewing on a button, painting a wall, scrubbing a floor, sweeping a floor.

I. Schoolroom Pantomime.

As the children become familiar with the school routine and with ordinary school equipment, there are many actions they can pantomime: cutting with scissors, picking up paper scraps from the floor, sharpening pencils, painting on an imaginary easel, wiping up imaginary spilled juice, drinking from a water fountain, playing a piano, taking off coats and hanging them up, putting on boots, washing hands.

J. At Home Pantomime.

These actions can be categorized to give the different activities greater meaning. Actions concerned with getting up in the morning: brushing teeth, combing hair, getting dressed, putting on shoes. Actions concerned with mealtime: drinking from a cup, setting the table, cutting with a knife, eating soup. Actions concerned with helping mother or father: dusting, carrying out the garbage, washing the car, mowing the lawn, washing windows. Actions concerned with getting ready for bed: taking off clothes, hanging up clothes, opening the bed. In this activity, as well as in preceding ones, some of the children may be allowed to guess the action being pantomimed. However, the idea of pantomime and some skill must be developed before guessing will be successful. At first have all children engage in the actions.

K. Show Me.

1. "Today we will choose our toys in a new way. You will be able to use puzzles, building blocks, and hammering sets now, but you have to pretend you have lost your voice. Show me what you want to use by pretending to use it. Who is ready to show me what he wants to use?"

2. "Remember when we talked about the things we like to do best after school? Let's act out the thing we enjoy doing best this time. Who wants to start? All right, Tony."

3. Present items used frequently during school routines: pencil, crayon, geometric inset, hammer, simple puzzle, book, cups, napkins. "I am going to hold up one of these, and I want you to pretend to use it." If the children have difficulty, provide hints or demonstrate. Repeat objects so that those children who were unable to act out the first time can try again.

L. Fingerplays.

Of course any of the routine fingerplays traditionally used by preschool teachers emphasize motor responses as well as careful listening and verbal responses.

Manipulative Materials

A. Blocks.

Give the child three blocks and tell him to make a bridge, a three layer cake, a sidewalk. Vary the number and shape of the blocks given the child to provide new and interesting building possibilities.

B. Cans and Dowels.

Give the child three cans or dowels of the same height but graduated in diameter. Ask him to make a tower with the thickest can on the bottom. Later he may accomplish this with five cans or dowels.

C. Jumbo Scored Rods (Creative Playthings, DJ101, $6.00 set, or can be made to your specifications by a local lumber yard; the homemade version will require finish sanding.)

Give each child a five unit rod. "Can you build a 'sidewalk' just like that one with the other rods?" If he, for instance, combines the two and three unit rods to equal the five unit rod, encourage him to find another way (five one unit rods or the four unit rod and a one unit rod).

D. Inset Cylinder (Creative Playthings, T620, 21, 22, 23; $6.95 each).

Give the child the cylinder block with the cylinders in so he realizes each one has a place. Show him how they are different, thick to thin or short to tall. Take the cylinders out, mix them up, and tell him to put each cylinder back in its place. When three or four blocks have been used by individual children, you may adapt them into a group activity. Place the blocks in the center of the table to form the outline of a square or a triangle. Put all the cylinders inside the square and allow a child to complete each block by choosing what he needs from the center "pool." Much trial and error will be required.

E. Self Help.

Self help frames are available from Creative Playthings and other toy companies. Provide the children with the actual materials used in self help: buttons, zippers, snaps, hooks, shoe laces. Use other articles requiring special techniques: a purse to open, a flashlight to operate, a watch to wind, box and jar lids to match and close.

F. Lock Boards.

A wooden board which features various locks, hooks, and catches may be made from items purchased in a hardware store. Lock boards are also available commercially from Creative Playthings and other toy companies.

Dramatic Play and Free Expression

A. Dramatic Play with Dress up Materials.

A selection of hats will help children pretend to be the person who would wear that hat such as a fireman, cowboy, fisherman, nurse, policeman, lady, or sailor. Help the children think of ways to act like that person. If the child is wearing the fireman's hat, suggest he put out a fire. Show him how he might use an imaginary hose to put out the fire.

B. Dramatic Play on Familiar Themes.

1. Act out stories with which the children have become familiar (*The Three Bears* or *Little Red Riding Hood*). Assign each child a part. Read

or tell the story slowly while the children act out the roles. Later they may be able to improvise simple dialogue.

2. "Let's make believe we're still at home. What do we do to get ready for school?" Encourage the children to make specific motions of waking, getting dressed, eating cereal. Vary the pretend situation: cleaning house, grocery shopping, working at school.

3. Nursery rhymes lend themselves to pantomime. Simple props such as a candle or a plastic bucket may be used for "Jack Be Nimble" or "Jack and Jill." Sometimes the entire class may act out the same rhyme; at other times they may take turns acting out a rhyme before the group. The teacher recites the rhyme slowly while the children act it out. Initially the teacher may need to serve as a model for appropriate actions.

4. Animal make believe. "Would you like to play a pretend game about a little animal? First, you must guess the name of this animal. Ready?

"It is not very big.
Its home is in a tree.
It has a long furry tail.
It will eat all kinds of nuts.
It is a —————.

"Good! You guessed that it was a squirrel. Close your eyes and pretend you are a squirrel. You are a baby squirrel curled up in your nest in the tree. You are tired of being a baby. You want to be a grown up squirrel like your mother.

"One day Mother Squirrel leaves the nest to hunt for food. 'Now is my chance!' you think. 'I'll climb down this tree and see what this big, wide world is like.'

"On the ground you look all around to see what you can find. Over

Motor responses express dimensional terms "very, very little" and "very, very big."

there is a big log. Wouldn't it be fun to climb up on the log and run along it? Ooops! You slipped! Back on the ground!

"What else can you see? Oh! Look at those pretty red berries. Are they good to eat? Ugh! Well, you weren't very hungry for berries! Then you spy a big stump. Off you go to play 'King on a Stump.' Be careful! You backed up too far and almost fell off your stump.

"Something drops to the ground. A nut! A nut tree is over there. You race to the tree and grab a nut. While you are busy eating, a big, red fox creeps quietly toward you. Just as he is about to pounce on you, a redbird calls out, 'Danger! Run, Little Squirrel, run!' Up the tree you go as fast as you can go.

"After a while the fox goes away. You climb down the tree very, very quietly. On the ground you look all around. Then you hurry from tree to tree until you come to your very own tree. Up you climb until you reach your nest. You curl your long, bushy tail around you. As you drop off to sleep, you think, 'Maybe a grown up squirrel doesn't have so much fun after all!' "

5. For a day that looks like snow:

"This morning when we talked about the weather we decided it could start snowing almost any minute. How would you like to play a pretend story about a little snowflake? Good! I thought you would. Remember, now, a little snowflake cannot talk. It moves about easily, lightly. A little snowflake would never clump, clump about, would it? Of course not. As you play this story, I'd like to see how many parts of your body you can move. Are you ready? Well, then,

Close your eyes and count to three.
A little white snowflake you will be.

The Adventures of a Snowflake

"High above the earth are many big, gray clouds. There are so many clouds they seem to cover the whole sky. You, Little Snowflake, are in one of these clouds. There are so many snowflakes in the cloud with you that you move restlessly here and there. As you move about, you keep bumping lightly into each other. Finally, the cloud says very crossly, 'All right, you snowflakes, if you can't keep still, out you go!'

"Out of the cloud you tumble, and you begin to float toward the earth. You float easily, lazily, down, down, down!

"Suddenly the wind begins to blow, and you float faster, here and there. What is that tall, dark monster below you? It seems to reach out with hundreds of arms to catch you. You try to float past it, but you can't. The wind is pushing you down, down. You land on one of the monster's arms and there you stay, stuck fast. You are on top of thousands of your friends who were caught there before you. You tug and you pull, but you cannot get away. Finally, you just rest quietly.

"You look all around. What can you do? Will this monster eat you? Then the wind begins to blow harder, and the monster's arms begin to sway back and forth, back and forth. Suddenly you feel yourself slipping. Woosh! There you go, you and thousands of your friends. Down, down you tumble toward the ground. By this time you are so tired you snuggle up close to your friends and fall fast asleep. The big, gray clouds are empty now, and they silently begin to disappear.

"When morning comes, the bright sun awakens you. You squirm and try to keep its bright light out of your eyes. After awhile the sun climbs higher in the sky and a shadow falls over you. Now you can see! The shadow is made by a big tree. Was that the monster who had caught you with one of its many arms? Just then you hear voices. You look up and you see two children running toward you.

" 'Oh, the beautiful, beautiful snow!' cries the little girl. 'I think I'll lie down in it and be a snow angel.'

" 'You can be an angel if you want to,' said the boy. 'I'm going to make a snowman. The snow is just right for packing.'

"You watch as the boy picks up some snow and makes a ball. Then he puts the snowball on the ground near you and begins to roll it in the snow. Soon his snowball rolls right over you and you are caught up in it. Over and over you roll, over and over. Now it is very dark because you are somewhere inside the big snowball. What will happen to you? Will you ever see the bright sun again?

"The rolling stops and you lie very still. You can hear the voices of the children and you wish you could see what they are doing. After a while you hear the boy say happily, 'My snowman is almost finished. I think I'll just push away some of the snow right here. Then it will look as though my snowman has legs.'

"Now there is light. Some of the snowflakes that covered you have been pushed away. You can see again. You see the children jumping

Motor Expression

around you as they say, 'What a handsome snowman! Maybe he will last all winter!' You feel very proud.

"Then the children go away, and soon it is night. You cuddle up close to your friends and go to sleep.

"When the morning sun awakens you, you feel somehow that things are different. The sun is brighter, warmer, and you seem to shrink a little. Then you, too, seem to be changing. All at once you become a drop of water and you roll down to the ground. You are no longer a snowflake!"

6. How do I feel? Pantomiming feelings may be more difficult than simple actions. Tell a brief and simple story to set the mood. Use gestures and varying tones of voice to help the story along. Include situations which involve happiness, sadness, pain, headache, stomachache, sleepiness, earache, heat, and cold.

Adaptations for Music Period

A. Songs with Motor Encoding.

Many songs in the ordinary preschool repertoire utilize motor responses:

"Up on the Mountain Two by Two" ("Let me see you make a motion, two by two . . .")

"This Is How the Father Indian Plays upon His Drum"

"Sally's Hammers" (One hammer, right hand; two hammers, left hand; three hammers, both feet; four hammers, nodding head)

"Did You Ever See a Lassie" ("Go this way and that," motor directions vary)

"Here We Go 'Round the Mulberry Bush" ("This is the way we sweep the floor, clap our hands, stamp our feet," etc.)

"Looby Loo" ("Put your right foot in, take your right foot out," etc.)

"I'm Very, Very Tall"

"The Wheels on the Bus" ("Go around and around all through the town")

B. What Song Is This?

Act out a verse to a song familiar to the children. After they have followed your action, ask them to identify the song. Finally combine the words, action, and music.

C. This Is the Way My Dolly Walks.

Use a doll or teddy bear for the children to observe. Manipulate the doll in various ways and have the children duplicate the actions: walking stiff legged, walking sideways, walking with a high kick, hopping. Have the doll assume different positions and move in those assumed positions: walk with one arm raised, walk with both arms raised; have the children duplicate the actions of the doll.

D. Original Stories with a Musical Referent.

Tell the children a story which fits a musical piece or record you are going to play. For example, tell a story about a little Indian boy who does a rain dance for his tribe so the corn will not die. He dances and it rains, saving the crops. Then play a suitable piece of music. The "Apache Dance" would be a good choice. Have the children pretend they are the little Indian boy and do a rain dance. Music which suggests storms or marching may be used in a similar way.

E. Musical Stories.

A familiar story or a teacher made story may be adapted to group acting and can be accompanied by simple chords and scales on the piano.

1. *The Giant in the Woods*

   One day a group of children are walking through the woods. All of a sudden they see a giant fast asleep (one child lies asleep on the floor as the giant). The children (children join hands with the teacher and walk) are afraid of this giant, and scamper behind some nearby bushes (children hide). One brave boy ventures out to prove that he is not afraid (continue to supply appropriate actions). Walking around and around the giant, he finally jumps over the giant and does it again and again. Finally he beckons to his friends to come join him. All the children come out and one by one jump over the giant. The last child to jump trips and falls on the giant awakening him. Again the children scamper behind the bushes. The giant smiles at the children and beckons them to come out; he is a friendly giant. The children all join hands and form a circle around the giant and sing, "Oh, he is a friendly giant."

2. "Did you ever pick a big, red apple from a tree in an apple orchard? I see a few of you have. Was it fun? Would you all like to pretend that you are going to the apple orchard? Well, then, we'll go. But first I want you to listen to this music. It will tell you whether you are to run, walk, or skip to the apple orchard. Raise your hand when you know how the music wants you to move. Good! The music tells you to walk. When the music stops, you will be in a big apple orchard.

   The Apple Orchard

   "Now you are in the orchard. There are many trees, and each tree has a ladder that reaches to the top of the tree. Under each tree there is a bag. Pick up the bag and climb up the ladder into the tree. Pick the apples one at a time and put them into your bag. When the bag is full, climb down the ladder. You have worked very hard and you are very hungry. Choose a big, juicy apple from your bag. Sit down under a tree and eat your apple. While you are eating, listen to the music that will tell you how you are to go home.

"Can you tell me how the music wants you to move? Right! Now skip away home until the music tells you to stop."

F. Moving to Music.

1. Moving to the beat of the drum.

2. Let the music tell you how to move (fast or slow, skipping, hopping, or marching).

3. Rhythmic movement with chiffon scarves. A rainbow assortment of filmy chiffon scarves, two for each child, is best. Records or the piano may be used for accompaniment. The children may use the scarves for rhythmic movements, but they also may use them to give impressions of actual events: birds flying, boats sailing, a tree in the wind, leaves falling, fire burning. The children may use the scarves to follow directions in simple circle games. "Put your scarves *in* the circle; put them *out*. Wave them high *above* your head; wave them *low* at your feet."

PART V

Verbal Associations

(Auditory Vocal Association)

Activities to Reinforce Associations of Opposites or Dissimilar Qualities

A. **Opposite Mode of Questioning.**

Use, as a matter of teaching style, an opposite mode of questioning or of making observations, regardless of subject matter. For example, assume the subject matter under consideration is fruits. Point out that:

A peach has a single seed, but melons have *many seeds*.

A melon is large, but a cherry is *small*.

The peeling of a pineapple is rough; the peeling of an apple is *smooth*.

A tree is tall, a bush is *short*.

A strawberry has seeds outside; an apple has seeds *inside*.

(The children provide the italicized information.)

The ordinary routine of the nursery school provides many opportunities for you to employ such a format.

When you wash your hands, they're wet; but when you wipe them with a towel, they get *dry*.

When you pour juice, your cup is full; but after you drink the juice, your cup is *empty*.

If you walk you go slowly, but if you run you go *fast*.

If I raise my hand or put it in the air, it's up; but when I put it in my lap, it's *down*.

B. **Opposite Concepts for the Felt Board (Beckley-Cardy Co., Instructo No. 33, $2.50).**

This set includes 40 flocked illustrations which can be used with a standard felt board. Although illustrations introduce a visual element, the exercise can be performed to reinforce auditory vocal associations. "Water made this car clean; mud had made it _____." The child supplies the missing word and goes on to find the appropriate pair of pictures which he places side by side on the flannel board. In some cases, a visual clue may be necessary before the child can supply the vocal response. This set includes opposites such as wet and dry, on and off, tall and short, empty and full, up and down, big and little. The illustrations may be removed from the felt board at the end of the lesson by presenting a different statement. The child supplies the missing element in the statement, locates the appropriate illustrations, removes them from the felt board, and places them in the storage box. This review (and clean up) is very useful for helping children who missed responses on the first presentation.

C. Opposite Picture Folders.

Collect magazine pictures which illustrate opposite concepts. Reinforce these pictures by mounting them on construction paper. Store them in separate folders which are labeled "Open-Shut (Closed)," "Empty-Full," "On-Off," "Few-Many," etc. In the Open-Shut folder we might find a picture of an open door and a closed door, an open window and a closed window, a refrigerator with its door open and a refrigerator with its door closed, an automobile with its door open and an automobile with its door closed, an open book and a closed book. The Few-Many folder might contain pictures of an almost deserted street and a congested street, a tree with only a few leaves and a tree with many leaves, a few blossoms and a field profuse with flowers, a few people and a large crowd. The teacher presents a statement ("When we drive the car, the door is shut. When we get out of the car, the door is _____."), and the child supplies the missing word and then finds the appropriate pair of pictures to illustrate the statement. Different statements can be used from day to day which will elicit slightly different responses and maintain interest but which illustrate the same pair of pictures. Later, the children may be able to initiate the statements.

D. Big and Little Box.

A collection of everyday items which come in two sizes but are alike in all other respects are kept in a large, sturdy box or plastic dishpan. Examples: large and small bars of soap, a small baby cereal box and a large baby cereal box, a small and large box of Jello of the same flavor, empty cartons from large and small sizes of toothpaste (same brand), a pocket comb and a regular comb, a standard toothbrush and a child's toothbrush, an empty large vanilla bottle and a small vanilla bottle, a large spoon and a small spoon, a large safety pin and a small safety pin, a large button and a small one, etc. These items are identified and paired by the children and the concept of big-little and large-small is reiterated. The comparative forms (-er) are stressed. Although the use of actual items introduces a kinesthetic visual element, there is much opportunity for auditory vocal associations. There is also excellent opportunity for pointing out qualities of likeness—both toothbrushes are made of red plastic, but the *size* is different; both cereal boxes are made of green cardboard and both contained rice cereal, but the *size* is different.

E. Alike and Different Box.

Keep in a large, sturdy box or plastic clothes basket a collection of items which have something in common (often their basic use) but which have obvious differences. Change the items or add to the collection from time to time. Examples: a pinch clothespin and a round clothespin, a plastic fork and a plastic spoon, a drinking glass and a cup, a watch and a clock, a pen and a pencil, a ruler and a tape measure, a mitten and a glove. Vary the presentation. Begin by asking a child to find two items used for drinking. When the child has found the cup and glass, ask why they are alike; then ask how they are different. The model for answering must be taught ("A cup and a glass are alike because _____ " ;"A cup has _____ but a glass has _____"; "A cup is different from a glass because _____ "). Later the child might choose one item and look for the related item. If children have difficulty finding pairs, begin by presenting a pair, making the appropriate verbalizations yourself, and then securing similar verbal responses from the children.

F. Special Animals.

Present pictures or models of animals which are special in some way. Ask the children to identify something special about the animal they see. (An elephant is special because of his trunk or tusks. A giraffe is special because of the length of his neck or legs or because of his unusual marking. A zebra is special because of his striped pattern. A skunk has a special odor.) Later, it might be possible to do this exercise without visual props.

G. Different Places.

Select two places which have obvious differences (city and country, home and school). "Let's find out if home and school are the same or if they are very different. I'll make a list at the board. First, let's think of all the things we do at home (go to bed, dress, eat, play). All right, now what are some of the things we do at school (sing songs, work on making designs, have juice, hang up our coats)? Do we do any of the same things at home that we do at school? Are most of the things we do at school different from the things we do at home?" Be sure to include some things which could happen at both places: hanging up coats, coloring.

H. My Friend.

Ask a child to stand up before the group and to choose a friend to stand beside him. Ask him to tell one way in which he and his friend are alike. ("We are both boys; we are both wearing blue jeans; we are both in school; we both ride the bus to school; we are both five years old; we are both wearing sneakers.") The second child is then asked to tell one way in which they are different. ("He is a boy and I am a girl. Her hair is braided and my hair is short. He is wearing boots today and I am wearing sneakers.") The first child chosen sits down and the second child chooses a friend to come up and the game is repeated. Encourage the other class members to add likenesses and differences to those given by the two children who are standing.

Activities to Reinforce Associations of Identical or Similar Qualities

A. Tell Me.

"Tell me all the things you can think of that I could wear on my hands." (gloves, mittens, rings, fingernail polish) "Tell me all the things you can think of that I could wear on my feet." (socks, shoes, stockings, sandals, sneakers, boots, rubbers, galoshes, skis, snowshoes, skates, slippers, thongs) "Tell me all the things you can think of that are red." "Tell me all the things you can think of that are shaped like a triangle." The question would vary according to the subject matter currently being presented to the children. Listing items on the board and adding a simple sketch is a good way to focus attention, even though the children are unable to read the list.

B. What Goes with This Word?

"Boys and girls, when I hear the word 'shoes' I always think of 'socks.' It's that way with many words. If we hear one word, it may make us think of another word that goes with it. I am going to say a word and I want you to tell me what goes with that word or what it makes you think of." Examples: bread, mother, baby, sister, brother, hot, rain, horse, eggs, milk, mouse, dog, smoke, fish, cake, work, thunder, ice, hungry, laugh.

C. Teaching Style Which Stresses Similarities.

Use a mode of questioning or of making observations which stresses similarities, regardless of subject matter. ("Why are a bike and a wagon alike? Why are a shoe and a sock alike? Why do scissors and a piece of paper go together? Why are a spoon and a fork alike? Why do a hammer and a nail go together?") Initially, pictures and models may be necessary to secure acceptable verbal responses (See E in preceding section, Alike and Different Box), but later the children can handle this kind of question on an auditory vocal level.

D. Rhyming Directions.

During exercises or music time present rhyming directions. "Stand tall. Face the wall." "Jump up high. Reach for the sky." "Spin around. Touch the ground." Later, give one direction and allow the children to complete the second direction by supplying the rhyming word. The teacher may make an appropriate motion to help supply the rhyming word. "Sit on the floor. Point to the *door*." "Give a loud clap. Give your neighbor a *tap*." "Stand up tall. Make yourself *small*." "Find your nose. Touch your *toes*."

E. Riddles.

Simple riddles created spontaneously by the teacher and related to the subject matter currently being presented are a suitable activity in this area. "I am going to describe an animal to you, and I want you to tell me what it is as soon as you know. This animal lives on a farm. It is large and has four legs. Sometimes it has horns. It has udders. It gives milk." (Animals, foods, items of clothing or furniture, vehicles, colors are appropriate subjects for riddles.)

F. Animal Talk (Mattel, Inc., approximately $5.00).

The red plastic barn with its pull ring produces the sounds of twelve farm animals in a random order. When the ring is pulled, the child can respond vocally with the name of the animal which makes that sound: "I hear a cow" or "A cow says moooo" or "A cow is in the barn." The pattern required for this response can be changed.

G. The Farmer Says (Mattel, Inc., approximately $5.00).

Various farm animals are pictured on a large plastic circle. When a child dials an animal and then pulls the ring, the farmer says, "This is a turkey." The sound of a turkey is then heard. The sentences vary slightly and are useful in encouraging a child to repeat exactly what he has heard—both the sentence and the sound.

Activities to Reinforce Associations of Class and Category

A. Name the Farm Animals.

Begin the activity by placing a farm animal on the felt board or by holding up a picture. "Can you tell me the name of this animal? Where would I go if I wanted to see a cow? Right—I would go to the farm. Is a cow the only animal that lives on a farm? How many farm animals can you think of? Suppose I start with Gary. Can you tell me the name of one farm animal? We'll keep on until we can't think of any more farm animals." The same format may be used for any category related to subject matter under consideration: tools, foods for breakfast, furniture, clothing, vehicles, items shaped like circles or triangles.

B. Furniture Movers.

Assign each child a room in a house. "Pretend you are the boss of the living room, Gloria; you be the boss of a mother's bedroom, Darlene; you be the boss of a baby's room, Tony; you be the boss of the kitchen, Gary; and you be the boss of the bathroom, Maria. Now, when I call out the name of a piece of furniture that would go in your room, you tell me that it belongs in your room. Are you ready? Sofa, stove, TV, eating table, refrigerator, crib, dresser."

C. Weather Game.

Improvise a story about the weather and the clothes we wear. "I'm going to pretend to look out of my window to see what kind of weather it is. Then I'm going to put on some special type of clothing. You try to guess what kind of weather it is from the kind of clothing I list. Let me see, what shall I wear to school today? Oh, my! I wonder where my raincoat is? And I guess I will need my umbrella. What is the weather like? Now it is another day and I look out my window. Oh, I will need my heavy coat today, and I guess I'd better wear my boots so my feet won't get cold. Where is my scarf, and I will need my mittens too. Can you guess what the weather is like? It is another day, not a school day. I look out. It's a perfect day for swimming. I'll put on some shorts and a light shirt and go to the swimming pool. I'll put my swimming suit on over there. Can you guess what kind of weather it is?"

D. Naming.

A general discussion of names and why we have them is an effective way to begin classifying exercises. "Name all the children that you can in our school. What would happen if people didn't have names? Why do we have names? Other things besides people have names. How many kinds of fruit can we name today? I will keep count on the blackboard. (Or, I will draw a picture on the blackboard of each fruit you name.) How many colors can we name? How many items of clothing can we name?" This exercise may also be done in reverse: "What are hot dogs, lettuce, bread, and apples? (food) What are

Roxie, Becky, Vanessa, and Penny? (girls) What are a banana, an orange, an apple, a pear, and strawberries? (fruit)." Another variation is to ask which word does not belong with the others. Example: "Dog, cat, horse, table. Why does 'table' not go with the others? What are the others? (animals) Bus, train, truck, house, car. Which word does not belong? (house) Why does house not go with the others? What are the others? (things that go)"

E. Downtown.

Create a pretend situation for the children as you tell a little story. "Everybody close his eyes and listen to the things I tell you about a certain place. When you think you know the place I am talking about, raise your hand. I walk into a building. I see shelves of canned foods. Then I come to a place where there are tables with bananas, apples, and other fruit. Vegetables are also piled up. There is a counter with many kinds of meats in it. Can anyone see in his mind the place I am talking about? What is its name?" Other places the children might recognize would be a gas station, post office, shoe store, fire house. Again, this exercise can be reversed. Set up a pretend situation which leads to "I went to the ___(name of place)___ and while I was there I saw . . ." At this point the children supply the items which they would see in this place, making the list as long as possible.

F. What Do We Need?

Verbally create pretend situations and help the children to list what is needed to carry out simple goals. "Your mother tells you that you can spend the night with your grandmother. You have to put the things you will need in a bag. What will you take with you?" "You are going to help your mother make pancakes (or some other food). What will you need?"

G. What Is It Made Of?

Another aid in teaching children to think in terms of similarities and differences is to classify by composition (as opposed to use, color, or size, for example). "Name everything in your house that is made out of wood. Is your house made out of wood too? How about your car? Name some things in school that are made out of wood." (glass, plastic, cloth, metal)

H. Songs on One Theme.

Songs like "Old MacDonald Had a Farm" have a classifying principle at work. Others can be adapted and revised, such as the Bus Song: the wheels go around; the driver says, "Sit down, please"; the people go bump, bump; the horn goes beep, beep. "This Is the Way We Wash Our Clothes" can be adapted to "This is the way we . . . . at school."

I. How Animals Move.

Mimeographed worksheets, picture collections, or blackboard sketches may be used. "I have given you a worksheet with four animal pictures on it. Raise your hand if you can tell me the name of the first animal. What is the name of the fourth animal? The second? The third? Some of these animals move very fast. Some of them move very slowly. (Animals might include a snail, a turtle, a deer, a rabbit.) Other forms of movement may be used: jumpers, creepers, flyers, swimmers.

J. Tell Me.

Prepare a word list according to a category related to material being taught at the time. Example: Fall list (seasons): leaves, pumpkins, storm windows, milkweed pods, pine cones, squirrels, frost. The teacher says one word to each child, and asks him to "Tell me about it." After the child attempts to answer, provide a model for him so that he can repeat the information in a more precise manner.

Activities to Reinforce Hypothetical or Inferred Association

A. Auditory Association at Storytime.

Auditory association activities are easily incorporated into a traditional story time. Questions which are not literally factual or closely dependent upon immediate recall from the story should be used. Examples: "Why did the dog find his way home before the little boy? Why was the policeman like a daddy to the little boy? What would have happened if the old lady had caught the gingerbread man? What might have happened if the gingerbread boy had found a little boat at the river's edge?" This type of question can be used with any story read to the children, but a great deal of practice will be necessary before the children can make acceptable responses. (A typical early response to a cause and effect type of question, "Why did the boy fall?" may well be for the child to repeat the effect, "The boy fell," as if in some way this explained the cause.)

B. Little Willy.

Create verbally an imaginary little boy (Little Willy) and use him as a focal point for examples from day to day. A hand puppet may be used to help create the character. Recount various events and ask the children how Willy felt. Examples: He fell down and hurt his knee. (He felt sad, sorry, hurt.) He found a nickle and bought a toy truck he wanted very much. (He felt happy, lucky.) He broke his sister's doll when he was angry. (He felt sorry, glad, afraid.) He ate a big dinner. (He felt happy, full, lucky.)

C. Finish the Story.

Collect large, interesting action pictures in advance and store in a folder. Tell the beginning of a story to which one of the pictures supplies a possible ending. The child listens to the teacher's story, finds the picture to complete the story, and then tells how the story ended. (Later, picture props may **not** be necessary.) Example:

"A boy's mother told him to go to bed. He said, 'I won't.' So the mother picked him up and carried him to bed. 'Now stay there,' she said, 'or I will get very angry.' As soon as his mother left the room, the little boy got up and ran out of his room. When his mother saw him . . . . . ." (Child chooses correct picture and verbalizes the ending.)

"It was a very windy day and a man was burning some boxes near a garage. He left the fire before it was out. The wind blew the burning pieces of cardboard over to the garage . . . . ." (Child chooses correct picture and finishes the story.)

D. What If?

To insure responses, limit questions, at least initially, to material which has been introduced in the preschool classroom.

What would happen if we forgot to put the covers on the paint jars?

What would happen if we did not put our names on our paintings?

What would we do if we spilled the paint?

What would happen if the music teacher let everyone play the piano during music time?

What would happen if we didn't pick up the blocks?

What would happen if we didn't take turns talking?

What would happen if we didn't put the bikes away at night?

What would we do if a child cried at school?

What would we do if we didn't have enough crackers for all the children?

What would happen if the bus got a flat tire on the way to school?

In most cases more than one answer should be sought. Accept a literal or obvious answer but encourage divergent answers.

E. What If?

To insure responses, limit questions, at least initially, to basic family and home information.

What would happen if an egg were dropped in your kitchen?

What would happen if you left a window open and it rained?

What do we do when the baby cries?

What do you do when your shoelace breaks?

What would you do if you cut your finger?

What would your family do if the car ran out of gas?

What would you do if you got on the bus to go downtown and found you had no money?

What would happen at your house if the clock did not work?

What would happen at your house if rain came through the roof?

What would happen if you tore your dress (shirt)?

As in Item D above, encourage different answers to the same question.

F. Let's Think.

Begin an informal little story, stopping at a crucial point with a question. Example:

"A family went on a trip in their car. They drove for a long time. After they had passed through a town, Father said, 'There has been a bad windstorm with a lot of rain in this town.' How could Father know that?" "They went on for another sixty miles. 'They have had no rain in this town for a long time,' said Mother. How could Mother know that?"

Similar stories can be created about any incident.

"What would happen if someone tied your shoelaces together?"

"What would happen if you left a hamburger and a dog in the same room?"

"What would happen if you couldn't open your mouth for a whole day?"

"John brought a little snowman into the house and put him on the table. Later, there was only a puddle of water on the table. What had happened?"

G. Things Which Grow Shorter after Use.

A blackboard sketch, a picture collection, or a mimeographed worksheet can be used. Pictured objects might include: eraser, ruler, candle, book, popsickle, scissors, fountain pen, lollypop, crayon, chalk. All of the pictures are of things which can be used, but some of the things do not change very much after use. The children mark or name the items which grow shorter after they have been used. After the items have been chosen, the children might be asked to tell why each item grew shorter after use.

PART VI

Visual Associations

(Visual Motor Association)

Perceiving Similarities and Differences in Material Presented Visually

A. **Frostig Visual Perception Program (Follett Educational Corporation).**

Many of these worksheets present visual similarities and differences in order of increasing difficulty. See the manual for further directions.

B. **Ordinary Classroom Routines.**

Many of the ordinary preschool routines give practice in visual association; for example, chairs, lockers, coat hooks, juice cups, and napkins can be labeled with animal seals, color tags, or geometric shapes. The child learns to find and use his symbol to recognize his possessions and to keep things orderly. A later refinement of this activity is to make a large wall name chart. Following the child's printed name appears his symbol (flower seal, red triangle); on his coathook, chair, etc. appears the same symbol. The child learns what his name looks like and how to find his symbol elsewhere in the room. At intervals the symbols are changed and a new name chart is hung.

When blocks are put away after play, they may be sorted by size and shape: "Put the blocks back in their special places. Put the square blocks here; the big rectangles go here. This is the shelf for the triangles."

C. Color Bunnies.

Paper finger puppets, which should be rolled around a pencil before being taped, are made in the colors being taught. At first, children should handle only two colors. Later, they may handle three or four. The children place the color bunnies on their fingers and rest their hands flat at the edge of the table. The teacher flashes a color card and the children pop up the matching bunny. (Teacher flashes a red card; children stand up red bunny.) The exercise may be varied through the use of a verbal command. (Teacher says "Red.") A story about the bunnies may also be improvised, and the children raise the appropriate bunny, whenever he is mentioned. ("The blue bunny walked down the lane and met his friend the yellow bunny." etc.) Colored pictures of objects may also be flashed (a red car, green wagon, yellow flower) and the children raise the color bunny which matches the color of the object.

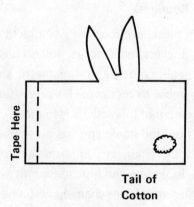

Tape Here

**Tail of
Cotton**

D. Coloring and Identifying Fruits (or other content, such as geometric shapes).

Mimeograph large, simple drawings of the common fruits (apple, orange, banana, strawberry, cherry, lemon). "Here are pictures of some of the fruits we have tasted at school. Do you remember the names of them? Do you remember the colors of these fruits?" Allow time for discussion. "Pick the crayons you need to make your fruits the right colors." Later, staple the pages together to make a fruit book to take home.

E. Which One Is Different?

Change the content of these exercises according to the curriculum, but the format remains essentially the same. Prepare a set of clown faces on small cardboard squares, on mimeographed sheet, or on the blackboard. All but one face have the same expression. "One of the clowns is different. Find him. How is he different? (happy, sad, angry) Now put all the faces that are the *same* in a row over here and put the other face way over here. That face is *different*." Later, three or more expressions might be used with multiple cards for each expression.

A variety of sketches may be used for similar drills: four apples, one has a missing stem or leaf; five daisies, one has two petals missing; four hats, one has a missing feather.

Building blocks may be used to create similar exercises. Make three arrangements built of three or four blocks. One arrangement is different. "Here are three buildings. Two of them are the same. One is different. Find the one that is different. Can you rebuild it so that it will be like the others?" (Bridges, layer cakes, walls, sidewalks, can be quickly built for this exercise.)

F. Match Patch (Arrco Playing Card Co., 29¢, available at variety stores).

This activity cannot be introduced until the children can identify a circle, square, triangle, and oval. Variations in play:

Visual associations: "Match Patch."

One child. Place the four key cards (heavy black outline of the four geometric shapes on white cards) in front of the child who then classifies the object cards. (Potato and egg object cards are placed beneath the oval key card; teepee and sailboat are placed beneath the triangle key card; balloon and clock are placed beneath the circle key card; box and block are placed beneath the square key card.) The child continues to classify until the 36 object cards have been placed beneath an appropriate key card.

Four children. Give each child one key shape card to use as his classifying card. The children take turns drawing from a pack of colored object cards in the center of the table or drawing from each other clockwise around the table, as in Old Maid. The object of the game is to place all nine object cards under the appropriate key card. There should be no winner; continue the game until each set is complete.

Two to five children. The four key shape cards are placed in the center of the table. The children draw from a center pack and place the object cards beneath the appropriate key card.

Initially you may wish to begin with fewer than 36 object cards, using only the more common objects. As skill in visual discrimination increases, verbal statements should become an integral part of the game. The child should say, "This clock has the shape of a circle" (or a similar statement) as he places the object card beneath its appropriate key card.

G. Geometric Assortment.

Cut squares, circles, triangles, rectangles, and ovals in two sizes and a variety of colors from colored posterboard. Store them in a three pound coffee can with a plastic lid.

1. Have the children sort according to shape. "Put all the circles in a pile here, all the squares here." Paper plates may be used as sorting containers to help control the task.

2. Have the children sort according to color. "Put all the red shapes in a pile here, all the blue shapes here."

3. Have the children classify according to size. "Put all the large shapes here, all the small shapes there."

4. An alternate method of presentation would be to paste a sample of each shape on a piece of cardboard. "Put all the squares on the cardboard

which has a square." Use a colored sheet of paper as a key for color sorting. "Put all the red shapes on the red piece of paper. The blue shapes go on the blue paper."

H. Pairs.

Pairs of objects identical except for one aspect are stored in a sturdy box. Examples: two pill containers, one containing seeds and one containing safety pins; two cardboard fruit trays from the supermarket, one shallower than the other; two white balls, one smaller than the other; two plastic cars, one red and one yellow; two empty gelatin cartons, one larger than the other. Give each child an object in turn. Have him tell the group what it is. Have him pick out the one that goes with his. Ask him to tell why it's the same and how it is different.

I. Opposite Concepts for the Felt Board.

See Chapter V, p. 57.

J. What Belongs in the Empty Square?

Cardboard sheets are marked into four equal boxes with a heavy line. (Shirt cardboards are suitable and of an appropriate size.) Silhouettes of various objects are stenciled in three of these boxes with crayon or felt markers. A visual relationship is established between the objects stenciled in the two top boxes. The lower left box is also stenciled, but the child must select an appropriate answer for the empty lower right box. He chooses this answer from five response cards. When the child chooses the correct response card, the visual relationship may be read from left to right or from top to bottom. The relationship may be one of color, of size, of object, of direction, or a combination of these. Example:

A red bird is to a blue bird (top row) as a red flower is to a *blue flower* (bottom row).

A large square is to a small square as a large circle is to a *small circle*.

A dog with his nose pointing to the right is to a dog with his nose pointing to the left as a fish with his nose pointing to the right is to a *fish with his nose pointing to the left.*

A simple way to use this activity in the classroom is to keep each card and its response choices in a separate manila envelope. The envelopes should be numbered in order of increasing difficulty of the contents. When a child attempts an activity, his name, the date, and the level of performance should be noted on the envelope. When he has satisfactorily completed this activity, he should move on to the contents of the next envelope.

K. ABC Match Ups (Playskool Mfg. Co., Playskool Matchup No. 7101, $1.00).

This game contains 24 pictures which are cut into two interlocking pieces. One piece shows the capital and lower case letter; the other piece shows an object which begins with that letter and also the printed name of the object. Example: B, b, and bear; F, f, and flower; I, i, and ice cream. The game is self corrective because the pieces cannot be put together incorrectly. A child need not know phonics to use these puzzles, since he can match the printed letter and the first letter of the printed word which corresponds. This is a fine visual discrimination to demand of preschoolers, but it is useful for advanced children.

L. Associative Math Concept Items (Creative Playthings).

These are useful in providing practice for visual associative skills related to number.

1. Match Mates. Ten individual wooden jigsaw puzzles, cut in half, are silk screened with numerals on the top half which correspond with

number of objects on the bottom half. Tops and bottoms fit only when correctly matched. (N125, $3.50)

2. Number Sorter. A simple, self correcting sorting toy designed to help four and five year olds understand number sequence. Two and one-half inch rubber squares have holes which fit over a corresponding number of wooden dowels on 12" wooden board. (N120, $3.75)

Perceiving Relationships and Clásses in Material Presented Visually

A. Clothing.

Cut pictures of clothes from catalogs and mount on lightweight cardboard or poster paper. Choose an appropriate size so the items are relatively in proportion. The clothing items may be sorted according to the following (or similar) classes:

Headgear (caps, hats, ear muffs, hoods, head scarves)

Garments for the upper body (shirts, blouses, jackets, vests, sweaters, neckties)

Garments for the lower body (skirts, trousers, shorts, slacks, tights)

Footwear (shoes, boots, rubbers, socks, sneakers, slippers)

Care should be taken to include items with differences: jackets with hoods, jackets without hoods; shoes with laces, slip on shoes; high boots, low boots. Capitalize on these differences when securing verbal responses.

One child or a number of children may participate, providing that enough materials are available. As a key to the sorting a large cardboard body silhouette can be used. Headgear is placed on the head, footwear is placed in a pile at the feet, etc.

The same clothing items may be used for various adaptations. Sort children's clothing (then separate boys' and girls' clothing) from that of adults (then separate men's clothing from women's clothing). Sort summer and winter garments. Encourage verbalization when a child becomes proficient at sorting. Vocabulary words to be stressed might include "hood," "plaid," "striped," "zipper," "buttons," "rubbers," "sneakers," "sandals." Appropriate questions might be: "How are rubbers different from boots?" "Would you wear this in the summer?" "How are gloves different from mittens?"

B. Moving Day.

Cut items of furniture from catalogs and mount on lightweight cardboard or poster paper. Choose an appropriate size so objects are relatively in proportion. If one child is to play the game, provide enough items to furnish one house. Ideally two to five children should play, and in such cases enough furniture to complete one house for each child would be required.

In addition to an assortment of furniture, each child is given a large sheet of cardboard on which is drawn a cut-away outline of a house. Outlines for the following rooms would be suitable: kitchen, living room, bathroom, two bedrooms. A garage and suitable contents (automobile, lawn mower, garden tools, bike) could be added later. The house plan should be large enough to contain the furniture without crowding which confuses the child. The sorting, not the placing of the furniture, should be the child's main task.

The child sorts the furniture by placing it in the appropriate room. Within reason, the child designates which room is the kitchen, etc. However, some logical choice should be required. For example, the teacher normally would not accept a kitchen located upstairs in a story sketch although split levels may have to be considered!

When the child becomes proficient at this activity, encourage verbalization. "This is a stove. A stove belongs in the kitchen." When you check the completed work, ask appropriate questions: "What pieces of furniture did you put in the kitchen? How many chairs are around the table? Is this a child's bedroom? Can you find an oval table and a square table?"

On a simpler and earlier level use a dollhouse and doll furniture for a similar exercise. Again, the children sort the objects according to the room in which they should be placed.

C. Playhouse (Childcraft Equipment Co., $1.00).

This game is produced in a playing card format. There are key cards which picture a specific room in a house: dining room, kitchen, nursery, etc. There are object cards which picture individual items from these rooms: a crib, a dining room table, a stove. The children classify the object cards of furniture with the proper room or key card. One child may do this sorting, or a group may play by dealing out the object cards around the table or by having the children draw from a center pile.

D. Who Gets It? (Dolch Materials, Garrard Publishing Co., $1.98).

The children match pictures of two different types of the same object. For example, an oval rug goes with a rectangular rug, an upholstered chair goes with a straight backed chair. Six children may play this game which follows a lotto format.

E. Playstore (Childcraft Equipment Co., $1.00).

This game is produced in a playing card format. There are six different stores represented on the key cards and 36 items of merchandise pictured on the object cards. The children sort the items according to the proper store. One child may do this sorting, or a group may play by dealing out the object cards around the table or by having the children draw from a center pile.

F. People and Their Jobs (Playskool Mfg. Co., Playskool Matchup No. 7106, $1.00).

This game contains 24 pictures which are cut into two interlocking pieces. One piece portrays a person at his work; the other piece shows some object related to that particular job. The pieces cannot be put together incorrectly, so the exercise is self corrective. Sample pictures are a milkman and milk bottles, fireman and hydrant and hose, barber and pair of scissors, mailman and bag of mail, house painter and paint brushes. The game may be played alone, or three or more children may play by distributing the people pieces equally. The other pieces are put face down in the center of the table. If the child draws a matching piece, he lays down the completed puzzle. If the piece does not match, he discards it. The next child may draw either the discarded card or a new one from the center pile. The game continues until all pictures are completed.

G. Animals and Their Homes (Playskool Mfg. Co., Playskool Matchup No. 7105, $1.00).

This game contains pictures which are cut into two interlocking pieces. One piece portrays an animal and the other piece shows where that animal lives. The pieces cannot be put together incorrectly and so the exercise is self corrective. Sample pictures are bird and nest; penguin and iceberg; camel and desert; mouse and hole in wall. Directions: See Item F above.

H. Store Windows (Beckley-Cardy Co., Instructo Classification Set No. 36, $2.50).

This set includes four store fronts and familiar objects. The children match the objects with the appropriate store. The objects are printed on flocked cardboard and are suitable for use with a standard felt board. Examples: hardware store front, clothing store front; hammer, coat, broom.

I. Go-Together-Lotto (Beckley-Cardy Co., Lotto Game No. 121, $1.25).

The cards matched to the pictures are related rather than identical as in most lotto games. For example, a letter is placed on the square which shows a mailbox; coins are placed on the square with a piggy bank; a dog is placed on the square which pictures a doghouse.

J. Go-Together-Pictures.

Keep in folders a collection of magazine pictures which have an association factor to be sorted by the children. Vocabulary drill should be added to the sorting, since many of these items cannot be named independently by the children. Examples: a tree and leaf (an apple, nest, bird, or squirrel might also match the tree, depending upon the exercise—so might a piece of lumber); hand and mitten (or glove, ring, or pencil); rain and umbrella (or raincoat, boots, puddle, rainbow, or mud); snow and sled (or snowman, snowsuit, or shovel).

K. Envelope Surprise.

Give each child an envelope containing small pictures cut from magazines and pasted on cardboard squares. The pictures in each envelope should belong to two or three categories. Example: five pictures of food, four pictures of objects with wheels, six pictures of children. Tell the child to put the pictures of the same kinds of things in special piles. "All the things you can ride on, all the things you can eat."

L. Pick a Pair.

Present each child with four objects that can be paired in a particular aspect: a can of beans and a can of peas, a milk carton and a pop bottle. Have the child tell why he put two items together as a pair: two cans of food, two things to drink.

M. Gummed Seals for Matching and Sorting.

Folders of gummed seals are available in numerous designs at most variety stores for about 15¢. Mount these seals on small cardboard squares for an almost unlimited number of classification games. A basic collection should include seals of fruits, flowers, farm animals, zoo animals, birds, fish, and butterflies.

Miniature wild or domestic animals can be used as keys for sorting the animal seal cards. For example, the model of an elephant, zebra, monkey, and lion are placed in a row in the center of the table. The children place the appropriate seal cards in front of each miniature.

After the children can sort the various bird or fish seals into appropriate piles they can proceed to a more difficult task—matching particular bird or fish seals to a *different* picture of the same bird or fish—those on the Wild-life cards, for instance (McGraw-Hill).

Flower seals may be sorted by color or by variety. They can be matched to another slightly different picture of the same flower, one taken from a seed catalog for instance, or to squares cut from appropriately colored paper.

N. Products.

Begin with a simple food, such as an apple. Discuss how it grows on a tree. Taste it. Have pictures of products derived from apples: applesauce, apple juice, apple pies. Show these pictures and discuss them. Some of these foods —applesauce and apple juice for instance—might be tasted. Later, these pictures are mixed with those of other types of foods (meats, soups, vegetables). The children are asked to put all the pictures of foods made with apples in one pile. They may be able to find other classes in the remaining pictures. The exercise can be repeated on other days: strawberry jam, strawberry shortcake, strawberry ice cream, for example.

O. Taller Buildings.

Give each child 15 small cube blocks. Ask him to make the blocks into buildings, each one taller than the one next to it. Initially, help the child to begin: "Here's the short building. It is made from only one block. Can you make a taller building? Fine. Now can you make a building from three blocks which will be even taller?" A stairstep of buildings should emerge.

Another day the stairstep motif may be presented by lining the children up according to height. A long piece of wrapping paper is taped to the wall. A mark is made on the paper for the height of each child and labeled with that child's name. Later, each child is asked to find his own line.

P. Classification Boxes.

Collect items which have a common classifying aspect (use is an excellent quality but color or composition—plastic, wood, paper, cloth—may be used) and store them in a sturdy box. Change the contents of this box from time to time. Sample items: a red button and a silver button, a tooth brush and a vegetable brush, a paper napkin and a cloth napkin, a plaid shoelace and a brown shoelace. The children pair these items, verbalizing the common element and pointing out the divergent elements.

To vary the activity, place one item from each pair into a separate box. Pass out the items from one box. Then pass the second box around the table and allow each child to pick the item which completes his pair. ("Look for something in this box which is like what you have. Good. Why are they alike? How are they different?")

Q. Seasons Felt Board Set (Beckley-Cardy Co., Instructo No. 263, $2.50).

Flocked cardboard pictures which illustrate seasonal changes: foliage changes, clothing changes, screen and storm window changes. These materials are suitable for use on a standard felt board but may be used at the table for sorting by season.

R. Opposites.

A number of opposite concepts can be developed with picture collections. Examples:

Far and Near: A series of pictures, such as the approach of an automobile, are presented to the children. "Here is a car far away. See how small it looks. Here is the car when it is very close; see how large it is. Can you put the pictures in a row so that it really looks as though the car is coming near you?"

Outside and Inside: Pictures of items which are normally kept inside (furniture, pots and pans, clothing) are sorted from pictures of items normally kept outside (cars, cows, lawn furniture, telephone poles, a tree). See pages 57-58 for further suggestions.

S. Which Things Make a Noise?

A mimeographed worksheet, pictures from magazines, or sketches on the blackboard may be used to present common objects to the children. The objects are named by the children. Then all those which make a noise are marked or sorted into a pile. Example: a rooster, button, dog, bowl, belt, bell, leaf, horn, hammer, piece of pie, truck. Similar exercises may be created to demonstrate hard and soft, hot and cold, and other classifying relationships.

T. Which Does Not Belong?

Give the child four objects (pictures may be used) and ask which object does not belong with the others. Sample groups: toy truck, toy airplane, toy motorcycle, safety pin; doll's dress, doll's sock, doll's shoe, crayon; cup, glass, tin can, pencil; pencil, crayon, chalk, scissors. Help the child to verbalize the category: "All of these are clothing. These can be used to write with. See, a crayon makes a mark, so does the chalk and the pencil."

U. What Do We Need?

Collect and mount pictures which show everyday work tools for the home. Two key pictures may be used to sort by: one picture shows a mother getting ready to clean; the other picture shows a father getting ready to work in the yard. Sample items to sort: rake, broom, dustpan, bushel basket, vacuum cleaner, mop, wheelbarrow, lawnmower, dustcloth. "Mother and Father won't be able to clean the house and work in the yard until they have tools to work with. If I give you a picture of a tool, can you place it with the person who will need it?" (Naming of the tools is an important part of this activity.)

Perceiving Sequential Relationships in Material Presented Visually

A. Picture Stories.

Line drawings or magazine pictures are prepared in frames of three or four to tell a simple story. Examples:

Picture 1—a tree (bare), picture 2—snow falling, picture 3—a tree with snow on its branches.

Picture 1—a tree with leaves, picture 2—leaves falling, picture 3—a bare tree.

Picture 1—girl with apple, picture 2—bite out of apple, picture 3—girl with apple core.

The children arrange the pictures to show the story. After the pictures have been arranged, the children should tell the story verbally. Old workbooks, preprimers, or other inexpensive books may be cut up to create simple stories of this type.

Initially, it may be necessary to tell the story to the children before they can sequence the pictures. Later, the children may be able to arrange the sequence without help from the teacher.

B. Which Came First?

A sequence of pictures showing a baby, a young child, an older child, a young man, an adult, and an older man are presented in a random manner to the children. "Can you put these in a row so that they will tell a story? Which came first?" Similar sequences might show the construction of a house, the growth of a plant or tree, a pumpkin being carved into a jack-o-lantern, a Christmas tree being trimmed.

C. Frostig Visual Perception Program (Follett Publishing Co.).

There are a number of worksheets in this set which show picture sequences. These may be used as indicated in the manual. They may also be cut into fourths, mounted on cardboard, and manipulated by the child to show a story. When the sequence is ordered, encourage the child to tell the story.

D. See-Quees (The Judy Co., series of 4, $1.00; series of 6, $1.25).

See-quees are printed on heavy board which is cut into 3" squares and fitted into a cardboard inlay. See-quees are available at a variety of levels and on a variety of subjects. Samples: Children's stories, such as "The Three

Pigs" or "The Gingerbread Man"; nursery rhymes, such as "This Little Pig" or "Little Boy Blue"; natural phenomena, such as the stages in the growth of a butterfly or a frog; everyday events, such as grocery shopping or going to school. Since all frames from a see-quee are identical squares, they are not typical puzzles. Rather, the skill needed is the ability to arrange the pictures in a story telling order.

PART VII

Standard Syntactical Constructions and Auditory Closure

(Auditory Vocal Automatic Process)

Using Concrete Materials to Elicit Verbal Automatic Responses

A. Miniatures and Models.

Miniatures may be used in many ways to provide situations for good grammatical drill. ("The father is *taller than* the mother. The baby is *in* the mother's arms. The children *are* playing on the floor. The mother *is* calling them.") Verb forms, singular and plural forms, comparative terms, and prepositions may be drilled through the use of manipulative miniatures. Of course, the child must hear the correct model and make the verbal response; he cannot be allowed simply to manipulate the miniatures. A child may be allowed to play freely with the models if he tells what he is doing. Then the teacher may expand his expression or supply the needed verbalization.

1. Miniature Toys by the Pound (Creative Playthings, B103, $5.50). Approximately 100 miniatures: animals, trees, houses, etc.

2. Bendable figures. These bend easily and may be positioned to walk, sit, or ride. Scaled one inch to 1' (father figure is six inches). Made of rubber, with plastic coating.

   a. *Bendable Rubber Integrated Community Workers.* Set of six includes worker, policeman, mailman, and fireman, DB319, $9.95

   b. *Negro Family.* Five members: mother, father, son, daughter, and baby, B492, $9.50

   c. *White Family.* Five members: mothers, father, son, daughter and baby, B292, $9.50

   d. *Bendable Rubber Negro Grandmother and Grandfather,* DB 450, $3.95

   e. *Bendable Rubber White Grandmother and Grandfather,* DB 350, $3.95

3. Stationary figures. These rubber figures are similar in size and appearance to those above, but they do not have the interior armature that allows them to be positioned.

   a. *Stationary Rubber White Community Workers.* Set of five: fireman, policeman, doctor, nurse, mailman, DB305, $6.50

   b. *Stationary Rubber Negro Community Workers.* Set of five as above, DB405, $6.50

   c. *Stationary Rubber White Family.* Set of five: father, mother, brother, sister, and baby, DB290, $5.95

d. *Stationary Rubber Negro Family. Se*t of five as above, DB490, $5.95

B. Where Is It?

Present two containers in two sizes (paper plates or foil pans in two sizes) and a red and a white poker chip (or similar objects). Place the red chip on the big plate and have the children verbalize: "The red chip is on the big plate." Place the white chip on the little plate and have the children verbalize this situation. Place the red chip on the big plate and the white chip on the table. Have the children verbalize: "The red chip is on the big plate." Ask the question: "Is the white chip on the big plate?" "No, the white chip is *not* on the big plate." Vary the manipulative situation and the verbal responses. Use two chips to involve plural forms. Later give each child his own set of manipulative materials.

C. Relationship to Child's Body.

This drill emphasizes common prepositions and relationships to body parts. Place a small object (pencil, eraser, penny) in relationship to the child. Supply a model. "The penny is *behind* your ear. The penny is *over* your head. The penny is *on* your head. The penny is *on* your nose. The penny is *under* your shoe. The penny is *in* your pocket. The penny is *under* your chair." After each statement ask, "Where is the penny?" and allow the child to repeat, "The penny is over my head." Later, encourage the child to answer the question without having been given a model response. The game may be varied by giving the children pennies and a block or a small doll. The children then manipulate the objects to follow the command and repeat the model sentence. "Put the penny under the block." Child: "The penny is under the block." "Put the penny between two blocks." Child: "The penny is between two blocks."

D. How Many?

Use counting books, pictures, and small objects to provide opportunities for the children to hear and use plural forms. "I have one block. How many do you have?" The child answers, "I have two block*s*." This activity can be done in conjunction with counting exercises. The child learns to say the number of things and what those things are: "I see four dog*s*. Here *are* six dog*s*. Here *are* three pig*s*. I see six *mice*." Similar activities can be used briefly throughout the day's lessons.

Using Less Concrete Visual Materials to Elicit Verbal Automatic Response

A. Arithmetic Readiness Vocabulary (Beckley-Cardy Co., Instructo No. 27, $1.95).

Use these cardboard cut outs with a standard felt board to teach language patterns, particularly comparative terms. The cut outs illustrate concepts such as many-few, more-less, big-little, young-old, long-short. Although this set is designed for arithmetic readiness, it can be adapted to create situations for a variety of language responses (using prepositions, plural and negative forms, for instance).

B. Flannel Board Cut Outs (Beckley-Cardy Co., Milton Bradley No. 7803, $2.00).

Use these multiple common objects (stars, birds, trees, flags, rabbits) to create situations on the felt board which require verbal responses that stress plural forms, negative forms, etc.

Counting activities in which the child says the noun pictured as well as the number presented are also effective. Examples: Child says "one *penny*, two *pennies*, three *pennies*, four *pennies*," etc., instead of merely counting the pennies by saying "one, two, three, four."

C. Opposites (Beckley-Cardy Co., Instructo No. 33, $2.50).

Use these felt board cut outs (or other pictures) to provide simple sentences which emphasize tense. Point to one picture and say, "The boy is going." Then point to the next picture and say, "Now the boy is _____." The children answer "gone" because there is no boy in the second picture. In a similar way, adapt simple two or three sentence stories for the opposite pictures.

D. Singular and Plural Pictures.

Collect pictures which show each object as a single unit in one picture and as a multiple unit in a second picture (one apple, two or more apples; one child, many children; one flower, more than one flower). Establish to your satisfaction that the children know the words for the singular and plural of each object by pronouncing the singular or plural of the objects and having the children point to the correct picture. "I will call out the name of some of the things in these pictures and you point to the picture I am talking about. Point to the *knives,* the *knife.* Point to the glass. Point to the child." If the children have difficulty making this differentiation, you will have to establish the correct labels before going on to more complicated activities. If the children can differentiate between the singular and plural words and pictures, go on to more complicated verbal responses. Ask questions which require changing verb forms, for instance, "What *are* the children doing? They *are* playing ball. What *is* the baby doing? The baby *is* crying. Where are the cows? The cows *are* in the barn."

Using Model Sentences

A. An Adult Model.

Do not insist on a complete sentence for all responses because an entire lesson can bog down in the constant demanding of a sentence form. This is particularly true when new material is being presented. However, after the new vocabulary or concept has been partially mastered, try to expand verbalizations into a sentence response. When a child gives the correct one word answer, say, "Yes, a *cow* is a farm animal." In other words, incorporate his one word into a simple sentence. Encourage him to repeat the sentence: "Can you say *all* of that?" Sometimes all the children can repeat the sentence to avoid self consciousness on the part of a single child.

B. Circle Activity.

For the first several days, until names are familiar, explain, "My name is (*teacher's name*). Will you say hello to me? Tell us your name, and we will say good morning to you. Good, your name is Tasha. Can you say, 'My name is Tasha?' We'll say 'Good morning, Tasha.'"

C. Music Activity.

Teach the first verse of a song with a repetitious format such as "The Wheels on the Bus."

"The *wheels* on the bus go *around and around*,
around and around,
around and around.
The *wheels* on the bus go *around and around*,
all through the town."

The italicized words change from verse to verse, although the sentence pattern stays the same. New verses incorporate new words but emphasize the same pattern. The children apply the pattern or, in other words, use the model. Other songs of the same type: "When Mary Wears Her Blue Dress," "Old MacDonald," "Put Your Finger in the Air," "Mulberry Bush."

D. Calendar Activity.

Emphasize the names of the days but repeat the same sentence. "Today is Monday, November first." A child checks the day on the calendar, inserts a number, or performs a similar tally check.

E. Juice Activity.

Later in the year, require each child to ask for his juice and crackers in an acceptable way. "Terry, would you like more juice." "Yes, please" or "May I please have more juice?"

F. General Curriculum.

Supply correct sentence models in all areas of the curriculum:

"This is a —————."

"This is *not* a —————."

"These are alike because this one has —————
    and this one has —————."

"These are different because this one has —————
    and this one has —————."

"They both have —————."

"————— does not belong there because —————."

G. Adapting Lotto Games to Model Sentences.

When playing lotto, matching, and classification games, present a model sentence to describe what the children are doing and why. For example, in a store classification game: "I have a ———— and it belongs in the ———— store." Most association activities lend themselves to similar sentences. "A *chair* goes with the *furniture*. An *apple* is a *fruit*."

H. Talking Time.

"Let's name all the animals (colors, vehicles, etc.) we can think of today. Each child has a turn and responds in a complete sentence. "A cow is an animal. A cat is an animal. A dog is an animal."

I. Tape Recorder.

Record brief lessons and play back parts to the children so that they may hear how they responded. However, before the tape recorder can be used effectively, the children must be familiar with the machine. A very limited use of the recorder is best at first:

Make a statement and allow each child to make the same statement. Play back immediately.

Ask a simple question. Allow each child to answer that question. Play back immediately.

The children may count pennies, up to five perhaps. Record the counting and play back.

Allow the children to give their names and to describe what they are wearing. Play back immediately.

These suggestions should not be followed at one recording session. Rather, use the machine daily for five or ten minutes.

Adapting Word Omission and Sound Blending Techniques

A. Riddle Format.

Blend a word as a riddle. Provide further hints or speed up the blending until the child can provide the word.

Incorporate sound blending into the regular classroom routine by slowly sounding any answer that the children are unable to provide. Instead of providing further information to help the child come up with the right word, as you would usually do, answer slowly: p - i - g, speeding up the sounding as necessary.

B. Farm Animals.

"We are going to pretend to be animals on a farm. We won't tell our full name though. When it is your turn, begin your name, like this: 'I am a c. . .' and the rest of us will guess the rest of your name." If the children have trouble beginning the game, suggest a beginning sound of an animal for each to repeat (sh . . . . . . , pi . . . . , ch . . . .). Play the same game with colors, fruits, or other curricular content.

C. I See Somebody.

Adapt the directions in A above to the names of the children. Sound the entire name slowly when an initial sound is not a sufficient clue.

"I see a girl named B————.
I see a boy named B————.
I see a boy named J————."

Familiar objects in the room may also be used: "I see a ch————. I see a cl————."

D. I'm Thinking of Something.

"Let's play a new game. I will tell you something about a thing you can see in this room. I will also make the beginning sound of that thing. Are you ready? I am thinking of something in this room that

1. is green. You write on it with chalk. It is the ch(alkboard).

2. is made of wood. You sit on it. It is a ch(air).

3. is made of paper. It has pictures in it. It has words in it. It is a b(ook)."

E. Rhyming Format.

"Can you make a rhyme? Let's see if you can finish these sentences:

Find your nose, touch your ———— (toes).
Take a nap, put your hands in your ———— (lap).
The little mouse ran into his ———— (house).
My little cat found a funny ———— (hat).
The big black dog jumped over a ———— (log).
The little bunny looked very ———— (funny)."

Use motions or picture clues to encourage responses.

F. Completion of Familiar Songs and Rhymes.

Use songs and finger plays with which the children are familiar. Repeat most of the words, omitting a word here and there for the children to fill in. "The wheels on the ——— go around and around, around and around, around and around. The wheels on the bus go around and around, all through the ———."

G. Forming Plurals.

Adapt casual conversation with the children to a word omission format. Allow the children to fill in the blanks as you say sentences. Examples:

"I have two hands and two ——— (indicate feet)."

"If I have one loose tooth I can chew with all my other ——— (indicate teeth)."

"I have one nose to smell with, but Tony and I together have two——— (touch both noses)."

H. Changing Tenses.

Adapt casual conversation with the children to a word omission format. Allow the children to fill in the blanks as you say sentences. Examples:

"We will sing in school today. Yesterday we ——— (sang)."

"I run when I play tag. Yesterday I played tag and I ——— (ran)."

"I rode on the bus yesterday. Today I will ——— (ride) on the bus."

I. Use of Books.

Books which follow a repetitive style are useful: *The Three Bears, Stop That Ball, Peter Johnson and His Guitar, My Ball of String, A Fly Went By, The Carrot Seed*. Either the illustrations or the repetitive style will supply the necessary clues for the children to respond to words or sentences which you leave out of the story. In some cases, a rhyme may be the clue.

J. Lotto Games for Sound Blending.

Use familiar lotto games in new ways. "This time I will not hold up the little card for you to see. I will slowly say a word, like this, 'ch - a - i - r.' You will look on your big card to see if you need that picture. If you do, say its name and I will give you the little card." Review the little cards first, holding them up and sounding out their names before actually beginning the game. Do not, of course, introduce lotto games on this level. Rather, exploit the visual level of such games first and later add more complex verbal and listening skills.

Helping Young Children Develop Language Skills

PART VIII

Auditory Memory

(Auditory Vocal Sequential Process)

Recall of Familiar Class Items

Review of curricular materials, such as class or category, provides a routine situation for evaluating and developing auditory memory. Initially, props (miniatures, pictures, blackboard clues) may be used; later these activities may be performed without visual clues.

A. Geometric Shape.

When reviewing geometric shape request a specific order of presentation. "Now, I want you to listen very closely. I am going to call out three different shapes. Then you will tell everyone those names and hold up the shapes in the order they were named. Darlene, I am going to call on you first: A rectangle, a triangle, a circle. Now you say them. Now hold them up—first, the rectangle. That's it." Give each child a turn.

B. Grocery List.

Initially use props for this game: an egg carton, a butter box, a soap container, empty tin cans with the labels left on. Place each item on the table as it is added to the grocery list. "I went to the store to buy butter. I went to the store to buy butter and eggs. I went to the store to buy butter, eggs, and milk." Individually and as a group the children repeat the list as it grows. Later, the children may be able to play the game without props.

Grocery Store is an alternate way of playing this game. Begin with three grocery containers. "Let's pretend this shelf is a grocery store and I am putting out some groceries. What have I put on this shelf? Let's name them: milk, eggs, oleo. Good! Now turn around and look at this side of the room. Don't look back. Tell me the things we put on the shelf. What was first? What came next? What was last? Good. Now I will change the groceries. Let's name them now: oleo, milk, eggs. Now turn around and look across the room. Tell me the things we put on the shelf."

C. Suitcase Packing.

At first use a small suitcase and actual items. Later, the game may be played without props. Example: Child One: "I am going on a trip. I will put shoes in my suitcase." Child Two: "I am going on a trip. I will put shoes and socks in my suitcase." Child Three: "I am going on a trip. I will put shoes and socks and a toothbrush in my suitcase." Each child repeats the previous list and adds a new item.

D. The Farm.

"The farmer went into the barn and saw a horse. The farmer went into the barn and saw a horse and a cow." Rubber animals or animal pictures may be used at first according to the procedure in C above.

E. The Garden.

"The farmer's wife went into the garden to pick beans. The farmer's wife went into the garden to pick beans and corn." Vegetable pictures may be used at first to stimulate responses; play as in C above.

F. Animals in the Barn.

Cut out a picture of a barn and paste it to a side of a small box. Pin the box to the flannel board. Use farm animals from a flannel board set or magazine cut outs.

"I have a picture on the flannel board that is going to help us play a remembering game. I'm sure everyone knows what this is. Right! It is a barn. Now in this barn are some animals. If you listen, you will know which animals are in the barn because I am going to make some animal sounds. I will make two or three sounds so don't say anything until I finish. Then I will ask someone to tell me the names of the animals whose sounds I made. If you are right, the animals will come out of the barn. Ready?"

After a child has named the animals in the right sequence, remove them from the barn and place them on the flannel board. Another child can put them back into the barn in the order in which they came out. Continue the game with another sequence of animals.

G. On Our Way to School.

"Did you see anything special on your way to school this morning? Good! Some of you did. Let's play a remembering game about the things we saw on the way to school. Terry, what did you see? (A squirrel.) Can you say, 'On our way to school we saw a squirrel.' Joe, what did you see? (A fire truck.) Add it to Terry's sentence. Say, 'On our way to school we saw a squirrel and a fire truck.' "

H. We Went to the Zoo.

"Can we play our remembering game using the zoo animals? This time we might say, 'We went to the zoo. We saw an elephant that ate peanuts.' Let's say that together. Tina, can you tell us another animal and something about it? (A zebra with stripes.) Good. Now let's talk about both animals. 'We went to the zoo. We saw an elephant that ate peanuts and a zebra with stripes.' What shall we add next?"

I. Vegetable Soup (or other food categories).

"How many of you like vegetable soup? Can you name some of the vegetables that we use in making vegetable soup? Good, you named quite a few. Now let's play a game to see how well you can remember the vegetables that are used in the soup. We will play the game this way: the first person will say, 'I made some vegetable soup. In my soup I put some tomatoes.' The next person will say that and add another vegetable to the soup. 'I made some vegetable soup. In my soup I put some tomatoes and beans.' The next person will add one more vegetable."

J. Fruit Salad (or other food categories).

"How many of you boys and girls like fruit? If we mix fruits together we would have a fruit salad. Name some of the fruits that might be used. Do you remember how we played the vegetable soup game? Fine! We'll play the fruit salad game the same way." (See I above.)

K. Memory Games Related to Other Curricular Content.

Adapt, especially during oral reviews, lists of related material to a memory game format. Animals and foods have been illustrated above; similar games might include colors, furniture, clothing, vehicles.

Recall of More Abstract Items: Digits, Letters, and Rhythms

A. Rote Counting in Proper Sequence.

Juice time provides many opportunities for simple counting. "How many children are absent today? How many cups (napkins, crackers) do we need?"

B. Telephone Numbers.

Use play telephones for the children to call each other. The teacher is the operator. Each child asks her for the telephone number of his friend. Give the more proficient children a longer series to remember. In order for the child to phone his friend, he repeats the series correctly. If he makes a mistake, the operator tells him he has a "wrong number" and gives him the number to repeat again.

C. Elevator Boy.

Choose one child as the elevator boy or girl. The other children are passengers on the elevator. Each child in turn names the floor at which he wants to get off. The elevator boy repeats these numbers and ends by saying, "Everybody off." Example: "First floor, second floor, tenth floor, thirteenth floor, everybody off." (Ideally, the children might give their numbers in order, but it is not necessary and the elevator boy may call the floors in whatever order they were first given.)

D. Prepared Tapes for the Tape Recorder.

For motivation and to save time and give individual help, prepare memory drill tapes. Vary these in content. Example: Record digits, beginning with only two numbers. A pause follows during which the child or children listening repeat the digits. Gradually increase the number of digits given. The same tape can be used for several sessions. (Material in addition to digits can, of course, be recorded and repeated in the specified order by the children.)

E. Finger Puppets and Hand Puppets.

Puppets help to motivate memory drills. The puppet may present a series of digits, letters, nonsense syllables, or words, and the children repeat the sequence. Later the teacher may present the material and a child may use the puppet to repeat the sequence.

F. Rhythms.

The children can repeat rhythmic patterns with coffee can drums, rhythm sticks, or hand clapping. Vary the patterns: short, long; short, short, long; loud, soft; etc.

G. The Giant's Garden.

Tell a story about a giant who needs children to help him weed his garden. Every child who walks past his house must repeat what the giant says to him or else he has to help the giant. As they pass, the giant (teacher) says three or four nonsense syllables (ro-de-dum, fe-ti-rap). The child must say them back correctly. If he cannot, he goes to a part of the room designated as the garden to hoe weeds. Increase the sequence or substitute words, digits, or letters.

Auditory memory—recall of directions.

Recall of Songs, Finger Plays, and Nursery Rhymes

Most preschool and kindergarten music and activity books contain materials which emphasize sequenced or ordered items. The following are typical and do not represent a complete list.

A. **Sequence of Number.**

"Ten Little Indians"
"Band of Angels"
"Three Crows"
"One Potato, Two Potato"
"One, Two, Buckle My Shoe"

B. Sequence of Items or Objects.

"Old MacDonald Had a Farm"
"The Farmer in the Dell"
"Sally's Hammer"
"This Old Man"
"I Know an Old Lady"
"The Mulberry Bush"
"The Wheels on the Bus"

Recall of Directions

A. Do and Tell.

Whisper a short series of directions such as, "Go to the door, knock on it once, and come back to your seat. Now tell us what you did." Be sure the instructions are not too complicated and that the main factor involved is memory and not the motor requirements.

B. Reviewing Directions.

When presenting a lesson on subsequent occasions, allow time for the children to attempt to recall basic directions before you provide instructions. "Today we are going to trace circles again. Tell me what we will need (paper, crayons, insets). Good, here are the materials. Now tell me what we must do first."

C. Fruit Basket Upset.

The children sit in a circle and the teacher sits in the center. Count off the children by assigning the names of four common fruits (apple, orange, banana, pear). The teacher calls out the names of two fruits. The children with that designation exchange places. When the teacher calls, "Fruit basket upset," all the children in the circle exchange places. Later a child may replace the teacher as the caller in the center of the circle.

Variations of this game may be used to reflect other areas of the curriculum:

Assign numerals one through four. The upset word is "Arithmetic."

Assign the names of four barnyard animals. The upset word is "Barnyard."

Assign the names of four jungle animals. The upset word is "Jungle."

Assign the names of four colors. The upset word is "Rainbow."

Assign the names of four geometric shapes. The upset word is "Shapes."

Recall of Story Content

A. Now You Tell It.

Tell a simple story and have the children repeat the events in the order of their occurrence. Help the children by asking "What happened after that?" Similarly, review longer stories which you have read to the children several times. Stories such as *The Three Bears, The Gingerbread Man,* and *The Carrot Seed* lend themselves to sequential recall; however, any story may be adapted to such a review.

B. Official Answerer.

Select one child to sit beside the teacher while a story is being read to the group: "Angie is going to listen to this story very carefully. She will listen for the names of the people in the story. She will remember what happens in the story. When the story is over, we will ask her some questions. If she can't remember, she might call on someone else to help her."

PART IX

Visual Memory

(Visual Motor Sequential Process)

Reproduction of Patterns

A. Can You Make a Necklace Like Mine?

When the children have mastered the small motor skills required in bead stringing as an independent activity not related to patterning, incorporate a pattern into a bead stringing activity. As you string a necklace, verbalize the pattern (a yellow bead, a red bead, a yellow bead, a red bead). Each child copies this pattern in his own necklace.

Later prepare a sample bead pattern on a string for each child to follow. Place the pattern string on the table before him. "Make your necklace just like this one. Look at the first bead, the one on the left. It is a red ball, so you will put a red ball on your string first. Good. Place your necklace below the pattern and check. Is it the same? Now look at the next bead. It is a blue cube. Find a blue cube in your tray and put it on your string. Check. Now look at the next bead." Go around the table helping the children to check

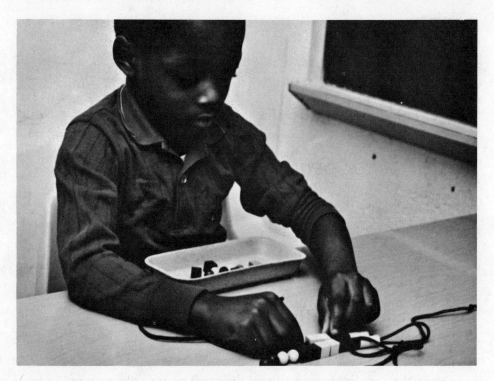

Visual memory: "Can you make a necklace like mine?"

their work and to verbalize the process. Allow the children to wear the necklace until the end of the period.

Bead patterns may involve size, color, shape, and combinations of these.

B. Paper Chains.

Begin with a simple alternation of color (blue and white) and build up to more complicated patterns. For young children use precut strips of paper so that the mechanics of cutting do not dominate the activity. Use transparent tape to secure each strip. Paste is too difficult for children to manage in this situation.

C. Necklaces from Drinking Straws.

This art project emphasizes visual memory and creates an end product in which the children delight. Cut drinking straws (colored or striped) into one inch lengths. Cut contrasting colored paper into one inch squares or other shapes. Use blunt plastic needles and crochet thread for stringing. Begin with only two colors: red and white striped straws and red and white one inch squares, for instance. A sample pattern: a segment of straw, a red square, a segment of straw, a white square; repeat.

Blue and white striped straws and blue squares may be added for a more complicated pattern. These chains may be used for room decorations (red and green for Christmas, red and white for Valentine's Day), or tied off in individual necklaces which the children take home.

D. Calendar Recall.

Cut the squares from an old calendar. Keep an assortment for each child in a separate envelope. Arrange two or three squares in a random order and allow the children to look at them briefly. Cover the squares while the children try to arrange their calendar squares in the same order. *A child does not need to be able to read numerals to play this game.* Begin with only two or three squares in a digit pattern.

E. Poker Chip Patterns.

Use poker chips for early pattern reproduction exercises because there is no element of reversibility with a round shape. Allow the children to look at the pattern while they duplicate it. Later, after allowing the children to look at the pattern, cover it with a sheet of cardboard and have the children reproduce it. The children may take turns making patterns for each other to copy. When the children have completed the pattern, a variation may be introduced: "I am coming around the table and when I come to you, close your eyes. When your eyes are closed, I may take one of your chips, add one, or do nothing at all. You then look and tell me what I did." (The child then remakes his pattern to the original design.)

F. Design Materials for Patterns.

1. Design Cubes (Creative Playthings, DT746, $6.00). These wooden cubes have four 1 color surfaces and two 2 color surfaces and may be used to create a number of patterns from simple diamonds to complicated designs.

2. Hexagonal design tiles (Creative Playthings, DJ115, $5.00). These rubber tiles may be used to establish a number of patterns to copy.

3. Rubber Parquetry (Creative Playthings, DT673, $5.00). These large, rubber triangles are easy for young children to handle and are a very quiet material for use in small groups. The removable circle inset permits greater variation in design.

G. Miniature Scenes (Creative Playthings, Miniature Toys by the Pound, B103, $5.50, or your own collection).

At first establish very simple scenes for the children to copy; an animal between two trees, for example. Later, arrange a scene, as on a farm (barn, fences, farm animals, people). Start with a few items, adding new items as the children become more competent. "Here is a farm scene. Look at it carefully to see where everything is. Is the calf near the mother cow or is it near the barn? When you shut your eyes, I'm going to change everything around, and then you will put things back the way they are now. Are you ready? All right, close your eyes. Now open them. Can you put things back the way they were?"

H. Flash (A three color flashlight is available from Creative Playthings, KQ476, $1.95).

Use a three color flashlight to create a color pattern (red, white, white; green, green, red, red). The child reproduces this pattern.

I. Memory Arithmetic Game (Milton Bradley, No. 7005, $1.00).

This game follows the pattern of the parlor game of memory or concentration. It is not necessary to read the numerals in order to play, and the abstract dot patterns and illustrations are particularly useful for young children. For preschoolers do not use the entire set. Begin, perhaps by placing three cards face down on the table. "Who can tell me which card has the picture of the cars? Good. Now which card has the picture of the pencils?"

J. Peg Boards (Beckley-Cardy Co., Milton Bradley No. 7615, $2.50).

Each child at the table should have his own peg board. Illustrate a pattern (an outline of a square done in red pegs, for example) and allow the children to reproduce this pattern on their own boards.

K. The House That Jack Built (Arrco Playing Cards, 29¢).

This game contains four sets of ten cards which illustrate the nursery rhyme "This Is the House That Jack Built." As the teacher reads the poem, each child arranges his cards in order on the table. Begin with only four or five cards.

L. Toothpick Pictures.

Use toothpicks to create interesting patterns for children to reproduce. Colored toothpicks may also be used. Samples:

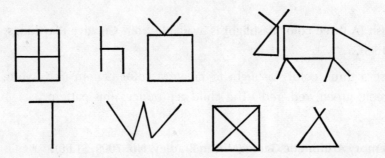

Popsickle sticks (purchased in large quantities) may be used for a similar exercise. The sticks are larger than the toothpicks and require less coordination to handle.

M. Alphabet Memory.

Use the letter dice from a game like Scribbage to form a random pattern. Children need not be able to identify the letters to play the game. After the child examines the dice he is given them and asked to reproduce this throw by arranging the dice as they were. The number of letter dice may be gradually increased from two to five.

A similar exercise which children enjoy emphasizes their names. Give each child a cardboard rectangle on which the letter cut outs for his name have been pasted. "Look at the letters. They spell your name. Now I'm going to give you more letters. You try to spell your name by putting them the way these are." At first, allow the children to copy from the sample frame. Later, encourage them to arrange the letters without a copy before them. (Cardboard letter cut outs are available from art supply and school catalogs.)

N. Geometric Shapes to Pattern.

Cut a large assortment of geometric shapes from colored posterboard. These are inexpensive materials to use for creating patterns (a green triangle, a red circle, a green triangle). The patterns may involve variations in color, shape, size, and position. Many children will go on to assemble these shapes into pictures: a clown, a house, a wagon. Allow the children some time for free play with almost all of the pattern-making materials.

O. Building Rods.

A variety of block sets may be used for these exercises. (Cuisenaire Rods are useful because of their size and color variables—from Cuisenaire Co. of America.) The rods may be used to create many visual patterns. Of course, there is the typical Cuisenaire staircase, but bridges, trains, cubes, fences may be used as patterns for the children to copy. "Look at the order of these rods. See how they go from a short step to a tall one. Now I'm going to mix them up and have you build the steps the same way they were." Or, arrange three or four blocks in a design. "Look at the way this building is made. The longest block is on the bottom and the two short ones are on the top." (Take the blocks apart.) "Now, you build the same thing." Later, reverse the design, placing the short blocks on the bottom and the long block on the top, etc.

P. Pipe Cleaner Prints.

This pattern project produces a take home art product which may be used for school announcements or for pictures. Materials needed: pipe cleaners, poster paint, and a somewhat absorbent paper. The end of the pipe cleaner may be used to make a dot or it may be bent in a number of ways (leaving a straight end for a handle) to create basic shapes (a circle, triangle, square) from which to make patterns. Sample patterns:

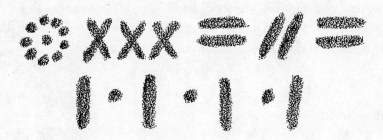

Q. Find the Missing Step.

Line up cans, dowels, or blocks to form a staircase. Tell the children to look at the staircase and then close their eyes. Remove one item and close the gap. Have the children open their eyes. Can they find the missing step? Can they make a space for it and insert it into its proper place?

R. Flannel Board Patterns.

Geometric shapes, letters, numerals, or animal shapes may be presented on the flannel board in a series which the children are asked to reproduce. A simple story line may be added to sustain interest in this activity. "These are the animals I saw in the forest: a white rabbit, a blue bird, a yellow butterfly, and another white rabbit." Or, "Here is a clothesline. I am hanging out my wash. Here is a pair of socks, a shirt, a pair of blue jeans." (Remove items from the flannel board.) "Now, can you hang these clothes back on the line just like they were before?"

Memory Games with Visual Clues

A. A Color Game.

Initiate this game with three very different shades of a color. Spread the three color bars, three shades of each color being used, in front of each child. "We are going to play a remembering game. Pick out a color bar from your pile. Study it very carefully and then put it down. Go across the room to that table where you will find another pile of the same colors. Find the shade that you looked at over here and bring it back. Put the two together. If they match, look at another shade very carefully and then go find that one. When you have matched all the shades, arrange them from the dark color to the light color." (Of course, all these directions are not given at one time.)

B. Let's Take a Trip.

Use actual materials. "I'm going to pack my suitcase because I'm going on a trip. I'm going to take socks, a pair of shoes, a hat." Allow the children to see what you put into the suitcase and to hear you name the items. Close the suitcase and ask the children in turn if they remember what you packed. Begin with only two or three items. Then begin to add items. "I forgot my toothbrush. Now I have socks, a pair of shoes, a hat and a toothbrush." Again, ask the children what you packed. Attempt to lengthen the list on subsequent days.

C. Variation on a Lotto Game.

Pass out the master cards from a lotto game. "Study the pictures on your card very carefully because you will have to remember what is there without looking. Try to look for things that will help you remember. Do you have all fruits? All animals? Ready? Turn your card over now so that you can't see the pictures. When I hold up each small card, tell me if you think it belongs to your big card. Who needs a red wagon?" (Children may need to turn over their cards from time to time for verification.)

D. Touch.

"I am going to point to a child. That child will jump up, go across the room and touch something—maybe the piano, maybe the table, a book, or anything in this room. Then he will sit down and I will point to another child. That child will go touch the same thing the first child touched and then touch one more thing before sitting down. The third child will have to remember both things that were touched before and touch them and then think of something to touch for himself before sitting down. Now watch closely. Are you ready?" Point to the first child and repeat directions as necessary until the children can remember the game sequence. Help by asking, "What did Joe touch? What did Gary touch?"

You can play a more complicated form of this game by touching the children who set the touch pattern. Mary touches the table. John touches Mary, the table, and then the pencil sharpener. Jane touches Mary, the table, John, the pencil sharpener, and then the floor. Harry touches Mary, the table, John, the pencil sharpener, Jane, the floor, and then a chair. (This game sounds more difficult than it actually is.)

E. Body Touch.

Touch parts of the body in a lengthening sequence: Head, knee, foot, ear. (There are a number of children's songs which can be used for this type of activity and which introduce auditory vocal aspects.) The children may play this game standing in a line; each child adds a new body part to touch. The teacher may act as a leader. After she has performed the entire sequence (four or five touches to begin with), the children perform the complete sequence.

F. Pencil Drill.

Use unsharpened pencils or rhythm sticks to perform a visual drill. Make a pattern with your sticks; the children follow suit. At first the children will be able to do only one pattern at a time, but later they may be able to do several in sequence. Sample patterns:

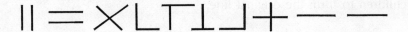

Incorporate this activity into music time.

G. Do as I Do.

Play this game much like the traditional game of "Follow the Leader"; however, all movements must be repeated each time a new movement is introduced. The original order must be kept, as follows:

Raise your hand.

Raise your hand and tap your head.

Raise your hand and tap your head and clap your hands.

Raise your hand and tap your head and clap your hands and jump.

This game may be played without verbal commands. The children observe the teacher and do as she does without being told.

H. People Patterns.

Place two children in a pattern: one behind the other, one to the left of the other, etc. Have the other children study the position. Tell them you are going to change the two around and they must remember where they were when they first saw them. The children then close their eyes. Change the position of the two children and have the others open their eyes. Choose a child to rearrange the children as they were before. Gradually increase the number of children used in the pattern.

A variation in play: arrange five children in a line. One child leaves the room after studying the line. Switch the children around, remove a child from the line, or add a child to the line. When the child is asked to come back into the room, he tells how the line has changed and rearranges the children to form the original line.

I. What Is Missing?

There are many variations which may be used in this memory game.

1. Present a miscellaneous collection to the children for their examination (a key, comb, pencil, crayon). After the children have observed the collection, one item is removed when the children close their eyes. At their second observation, the children are asked to identify the missing object. An object might be added, and the children asked to tell how the collection has changed now. From time to time the items in the collection should be changed.

2. Place several colored blocks or beads on the table. The children pretend these are pieces of candy and close their eyes. The teacher taps one child who opens his eyes and "eats" a piece of candy (holds it in his fist). Then all the children are told to open their eyes and tell which piece of candy has been eaten (the red one, the green one). For added fun, the children may guess which child "ate" the piece of candy.

3. Seat the children in a circle and direct them to close their eyes. Tap two or three children and direct them to leave the room. The others then

open their eyes and name the missing children, if they can. They should also tell where they were sitting in the circle. The children who left are called back in and take their original places in the circle.

4. Empty food containers are arranged in a line on the table. (A story line explains that this is what we are going to buy at the store.) The children then close their eyes while an item is removed. When they open their eyes, they are to identify the missing item. Again, more than one item may be removed or an item may be added to the assortment.

5. Doll furniture is arranged in a room. (A shoe box can serve as a "room.") One child leaves the room and one or two pieces of furniture are re-arranged. When the child returns, he is to identify the changes and re-arrange the furniture. Again, items of furniture may be added or removed from those in the room to change the response.

PART X

Visual Closure

A. Shape Puzzles.

Puzzles in which each piece represents a complete shape are particularly useful as simple closure exercises.

1. Fit-a-space (Beckley-Cardy Co., No. FSI and ASD, $3.50 each). Forty-eight pieces in 12 different shapes to fit into 16 colored rubber discs; 26 animals fit into 8″ x 8″ panels.

2. Puzzle blocks (Childcraft Equip. Co., 7M357, $2.00). Building blocks with inserts of familiar shapes (truck, horse, cat, girl) which can be fitted into the blocks or can stand alone.

3. Lift out object puzzles (Creative Playthings, No. DT747, $2.50). This plywood puzzle features removable pieces (a dog, tree, shoe) with knobs. These pieces may be lined up on a groove on the puzzle board.

4. Lift out transportation puzzle (Creative Playthings, DT736, $2.50). This wooden puzzle features removable pieces with knobs. The pieces represent an assortment of cars and trucks.

5. Shape sorting box (Creative Playthings, DQ949, $5.00). Five differently shaped holes are in the top of this wooden box, and five brightly painted, differently shaped wooden blocks can be dropped into the box through the holes. Each hole accepts only its corresponding shape.

6. Rubber stand up puzzles (Creative Playthings: Transportation, DT501, $2.25; Animals, DT503, $2.25; Family, DT504, $2.25). Each removable rubber piece in these puzzles is a unit and will stand by itself. When replaced in its wooden frame, each rubber piece stands out in slight relief.

7. Graded circles, squares, triangles (Creative Playthings, DN100, $3.75). The graded shapes are made of rubber and fit into corresponding indentations in a wooden slide-cover box.

B. Domino Halves Puzzle (Creative Playthings, R 17, $1.95).

Each domino sized card pictures the body of one animal at one end and the head of another animal at the other. Children select matching cards, building in domino fashion. The game may be played alone as in solitaire. With a small group, deal out the cards and complete the puzzle, taking turns around the table. After the puzzle has been completed, vocal activities may follow: The children can name the animals formed, imitate their sounds, tell where they live and what they eat.

C. Mix 'n Match (Arrco Playing Cards, 29¢).

These cards picture various circus animals and characters (clown, barker, seal, lion). Each character is divided into thirds; the head is on one card, the body is on the second card, and the feet are on the third card. The children find the proper match, either alone or as a small group game.

D. Go Together Animal Cards (Creative Playthings, DA308, $1.00).

Each animal picture is presented on two cards. The child matches the top of each animal with the correct bottom half. The cards may be used by one child or in small group play.

Home made variations of this game provide opportunities for further drill related to specific curricula units. Paste partial pictures of common animals on cardboard (pig, fish, dog, sheep). Begin in an informal manner: "Boys and girls, this morning we are going to play an animal game. You know the names of many animals, don't you? If I showed you a picture of a cow, you would say right away, 'That is a cow.' Now, suppose I show you a picture of part of a cow. Do you think you would still know it was a cow? Would you like to try? I will give each of you a picture of part of an animal. When you can say the name of the animal, raise your hand."

Similarly, paste pictures of "jumbled" or "fractured" animals cut from magazines or draw such sketches on the blackboard (the head of an elephant and the body of a zebra, the head of a rabbit and the body of a dog, a cat with a fish's tail). "Here is a funny looking animal. He has a head of one animal and the body of another animal. Who can tell me the animals that made up this picture? Which animal has a head like this?"

E. Etch-a-Sketch (Available from most toy and department stores, approximately $3.00).

Young children cannot create realistic pictures but can make interesting abstractions in which pictures "can be seen." This toy can be used also for practice in motor coordination and left and right identification.

F. Sewing Cards.

These cards are available on cardboard or on pressed board from dime stores and toy catalogs and may be used as an introduction to dot-to-dot drawing, a more difficult closure activity.

G. Dot-to-Dot Materials.

Prepare simple dot-to-dot drawings relevant to material currently being studied (fruits, geometric shapes, vehicles, animals). The drawings should be simple in outline and large in format so that coloring them is not an impossible or tedious task for young children. Most commercially available dot-to-dot material is too difficult for preschool children.

H. Finger Painting.

These constantly changing pictures constitute an art activity which relates to visual closure. Pour a small pool of liquid starch on finger painting paper. Add a bit of powdered poster paint for an effective and inexpensive method of finger painting.

I. Eye Dropper Paintings.

Materials needed: five eye droppers, poster paint in small jars or shallow pans (two to five colors, depending upon the control of the children), and absorbent paper. Help each child to fold his paper in half and to open it flat. The children drop paint in a random pattern on the right hand half of the paper only. Care should be taken to get some paint near the fold line. After several colors and a generous amount of paint have been used, fold the left hand half of the paper over and gently press the top surface flat. When the paper is opened, the wet right hand side will have printed on the dry left hand side. The results are interesting and encourage speculation. The most frequently produced picture is a giant butterfly.

Visual closure: domino halves puzzle matches animal heads and tails.

J.   String Paintings.

Materials needed: pieces of string, poster paint in small jars, and newsprint. Help each child to fold his paper in half and open it flat. The children drop the pieces of string into the jars of paint, holding the clean tag end for removing the string. After the strings have absorbed paint, pull them from the jar and place them in a random squiggle pattern on the right hand side of the paper. Fold the left hand half of the paper back over and place a pile of books on top. Now pull the tag ends of the string out. When the paper is reopened, the wet right hand side will have printed on the dry left hand side. The colored strings will have spread the paint and will have tangled with each other to produce rather complicated and well shaped pictures. Flying birds and leaves or flowers often result, but many other forms emerge.

Precut geometric shapes are used to design pictures.

K. Put Together Pictures.

Give the children the precut component parts to make a person or familiar animal. Without seeing a completed picture, the children are to assemble the parts in the correct fashion. The pieces may then be pasted on a paper or put together with brads. Exercises might involve assembling a man: head, body, arms, legs; a house: roof, sides, windows, chimney, door; the parts of a plant; or a rabbit. Ask the child, "Can you tell me what this is now, before you put it together? What would this be? (pointing to a piece) Put it together and see if you are right."

L. Geometric Pictures.

Give the children an assortment of precut geometric shapes in a variety of sizes and colors. Direct them to make pictures from these (a balloon, a house, a flower). Crayons may be used to provide detail later. Interesting variations are possible: shapes cut from black and white paper may be pasted on colored paper, producing an abstract or silhouette effect; shapes cut from colored paper may be pasted on black paper, a rather dramatic background. This exercise may also be performed at the felt board with felt shapes or with a pounding board, geometric wooden pieces, and a hammer and nails.

M. Shadow Pictures.

Collect pictures of simple objects such as a ball, tree, cube. Make "shadows" to fit these. "Can you put each picture with its shadow?"

N. Shadow Lotto (Childcraft Equipment Co., $1.00).

This typical lotto game presents all pictures in black silhouette rather than the usual picture format.

O. Goat (Milton Bradley Co., No. 7009, $1.50).

"Goat" is a beginner's card game in which the playing cards are sections of animal illustrations. The players trade cards from their hands and pair them up to complete the pictures.

P. Raggedy Ann (Milton Bradley Co., No. 4809, $1.00).

The players complete Raggedy Ann's picture by obtaining cards which match the pictures on a spinner.

Q. Finishing Patterns.

Suitable materials: rubber or wooden parquetry, fractional pies, plastic pegs and peg boards, felt board pieces, building blocks. Present an incomplete form and ask the children what piece or pieces are needed to finish the pattern. After the children have verbalized their decision, they choose the necessary piece or pieces to check their answer and to determine whether or not they have actually "closed" the pattern. A color pattern may be superimposed upon a geometric pattern to increase the difficulty of the exercise. "Look at this shape. It isn't quite finished. Can you finish it?" For example:

R. Incomplete Pictures.

Use mimeographed sheets or blackboard drawings to present a variety of incomplete pictures. "Here are some faces. Something is missing from each one. This one has no nose; this one has no eyes. What is missing on this one? Yes, draw a mouth on it."

"Twin" pictures may be made for many subjects. The children examine the complete twin and then look at the incomplete twin to determine what is missing. On simple pictures the missing items may be drawn in; on more complicated drawings the response is only verbal. Later eliminate the twin idea and present the children with the incomplete picture only—a dog minus his ears, a house without a door. The children name the missing elements.

Use mimeographed sheets or blackboard drawings which show the incomplete picture as well as the element necessary for its completion for matching exercises: a bucket without a handle, half a pair of scissors, a car with a missing wheel, a baby bottle without a nipple. The missing elements, together with other choices, are drawn on the other half of the sheet: a handle, half a pair of scissors, a nipple, a wheel. The children draw a line from the car to its wheel.

What's Missing Lotto (Creative Playthings, AA296, $1.00) follows a similar pattern. Each of the six playing cards shows a familiar scene (playground, farm, grocery store) in which there are missing elements (a shoe, a wheel). The missing elements are printed on the small lotto cards and matched with the correct playing card.

S. Draw a Picture from a Basic Form.

Draw a basic form on the blackboard and make additions to that form until a recognizable object emerges (a fish from an oval). Ask the children to identify the picture as soon as they can. Later they are given the same basic shape and asked to draw a similar picture. (Balloons or a snowman from circles, a house from a square, a tree from a triangle, a mouse from an oval.)

T. The Frostig Program of Visual Perception (Follett Publishing Co.).

A number of the practice sheets in this set may be used for closure drill. See Teacher's Manual for suggestions.

U. Kaleidoscope (available with an empty head at most dime stores for about $1.00).

Show an assortment of small objects to the children: a paper clip, button, rubber band, bit of colored paper, snap. After the children have examined and identified the objects, remove them from sight. Place one of these objects in the empty kaleidoscope head and allow the children to guess which object they are seeing through the kaleidoscope. The results are not as simple to identify as one would suppose. When the children can identify one object correctly, insert two or three items at the same time. Three objects produce a rather complicated abstraction when seen through the prism of a kaleidoscope.

The Teleidescope (Creative Playthings, AS564, $3.00) produces similar results but lacks the factor of control. The child may focus the teleidescope on any object in the room and see it prismatically fractured. Again, the patterns are striking and the identification is not simple, even when the child knows what he is looking at.

V. Scribble Pictures and Hidden Pictures.

Mimeograph large, relatively simple scribble pictures. If the drawing is large enough, the children may color in the objects they have identified (hidden butterflies, balloons, or flowers).

A more abstract scribble can be made by having the teacher (later the child) scribble an open line pattern with a black marker or a black crayon. The child then colors in the segments. A "stained glass" results. With some care on the part of the teacher's scribbling, basic shapes or simple objects can also emerge. The child can be told what to look for in his scribble. "Find three hidden balloons in this scribble and color them red. Find a banana in this scribble and color it yellow."

Similar pictures may be made by asking the children to color only the spaces which have a dot in them. Examples: a bird emerges among the leaves when each space with a dot in it is colored blue and each space without a dot is colored green; a turtle emerges among the stones when each space with a dot is colored green and each space without a dot is colored brown.

Superimposed figures may be used in this fashion. For example, geometric shapes may be superimposed, overlapping a circle, square, and triangle. The child is asked to find a specific shape and outline it or color it with his crayon. Pictures of superimposed objects may also be used.

W. Paper Plate Faces.

Give each child a paper plate to represent a face and precut features for this face. The children paste the features appropriately on the face. For young children, the mouth or an eye might be prepasted to help orient the child.

X. Composite Blackboard Drawing.

Begin a drawing on the blackboard and ask each child to add a detail to help complete the picture. "We are going to draw a person on the board today. I'll make the head. Then it's Dick's turn to put on something that a person must have." Houses, dogs, and flowers are other subjects for composite drawings. Use colored chalk to stimulate interest.

Y. What Is It?

Cut up magazine pictures of relatively simple objects and paste them in a random fashion on shirt cardboards (a telephone, automobile, airplane, boy on a bike). The child looks at the pasted pieces and is asked to identify the picture. He cannot arrange the pieces since they are pasted down in their "broken" fashion.

Z. Half and Half.

Prepare simple cut out silhouettes from a folded piece of paper. Ask the child to identify the object before it is unfolded. "I am going to cut a shape out of this paper. You watch and see if you can guess what shape it will be.

You can't see all of it yet, but what do you think it will be?" Open the fold so the children may confirm their answers. Give the shape to the child who guessed correctly first. Help all children so that each child will have some shapes. Sample items: a heart, tree, flower, gingerbread man or person, familiar geometric shapes.

Appendix

Listing of Sources

Acadia Press, Inc.
1144 South Main Avenue
Scranton, Pennsylvania 18504

Beckley-Cardy Co.
1900 Narragansett Avenue
Chicago, Illinois 60639

Childcraft Equipment Co., Inc.
155 East 23rd Street
New York, New York 10010

Creative Playthings, Inc.
Princeton, New Jersery 08540

Cuisenaire Company of America, Inc.
235 East 50th Street
New York, New York 10022

Follett Publishing Company
1010 West Washington Boulevard
Chicago, Illinois 60607

Garrard Publishing Co.
1607 N. Market
Champaign, Illinois 61820

Golden Press
850 Third Avenue
New York, New York 10022

The Judy Company
310 N. Second St.
Minneapolis, Minnesota 55401

McGraw-Hill
Educational Aids Division
330 West 42nd Street
New York, New York 10036

Milton Bradley Co.
74 Park Street
Springfield, Massachusetts 01105

National Wildlife Federation
1412 16th St., N.W.
Washington, D.C. 20036

Playskool Manufacturing Co.
3720 N. Kedzie Avenue
Chicago, Illinois 60618

Scott, Foresman and Company
1900 East Lake Avenue
Glenview, Illinois 60025

Teachers Publishing Corporation
Darien, Connecticut 16820